P9-DXO-073

Selected Poems from *Les Fleurs du mal*

CHARLES BAUDELAIRE

Selected Poems from *Les Fleurs du mal*

A BILINGUAL EDITION

English Renderings and Notes by Norman R. Shapiro

Foreword by Willis Barnstone

Engravings by David Schorr

THE UNIVERSITY OF CHICAGO PRESS *Chicago and London*

NORMAN R. SHAPIRO is professor of Romance languages and literatures at
Wesleyan University. Among his many translations are *Fifty Fables of La Fontaine*
(1988), *The Fabulists French: Verse Fables of Nine Centuries* (1992), which was the
winner of the ALTA Distinguished Translation Award for 1993, and *Four Farces
by Georges Feydeau*, published by the University of Chicago Press in 1971 and
nominated for the National Book Award in the translations category.

DAVID SCHORR'S prints are shown regularly at the Mary Ryan Gallery, New York.
His illustrations have appeared in *The New Republic* and in many books, including
four with Norman Shapiro.

Frontispiece: "Portrait of Baudelaire," © 1998 by David Schorr.

The University of Chicago Press, Chicago 60637
The University of Chicago Press, Ltd., London
© 1998 by The University of Chicago
Engravings © 1998 by David Schorr
All rights reserved. Published 1998
Printed in the United States of America
07 06 05 04 03 02 01 00 99 98   1 2 3 4 5
ISBN: 0-226-03925-0 (cloth)

Library of Congress Cataloging-in-Publication Data

Baudelaire, Charles, 1821–1867.
    [Fleurs du mal. English & French. Selections]
    Selected poems from Les fleurs du mal : a bilingual edition /
Charles Baudelaire ; English renderings and notes by Norman R.
Shapiro ; foreword by Willis Barnstone ; engravings by David Schorr.
        p.   cm.
    Includes bibliographical references and index.
    ISBN 0-226-03925-0 (cloth : alk. paper)
    I. title.
PQ2191.F62E5   1998
841'.8—dc21   97-38283
                                                                    CIP

FOR EVELYN

Contents

viii

ILLUSTRATIONS

FOREWORD

With the publication in 1857 of *Les Fleurs du mal* (The Flowers of Evil) by Charles Baudelaire, modern poetry began. Baudelaire's rivals for being the grand maker of the modern were Walt Whitman, who in 1855 published the first edition of *Leaves of Grass*, and Emily Dickinson, whose poems, as befitted the last of these outsiders, were not published until 1880, four years after her death. Baudelaire's volume was publicly condemned as obscene, and six of its poems were suppressed, Whitman paid for his own private publication of *Leaves;* and Dickinson did not have a book during her lifetime. The titles that the "decadent" French poet and the "rough" American male poet gave to their books are identical in rhetorical structure: *Flowers of Evil* and *Leaves of Grass*. But one is a mirror image of the other: in contrast to the artifice of rich French *flowers*, we have plain American *leaves;* for destructive *evil* and *disease*, we have modest but vital, healthy *grass*. As for Emily Dickinson's title, she had none. Her revolution against society took place privately in her attic. These three writers also share a curious epithet: "one-book" poets. All their lives they elaborated a single, expanding bible, *Les Fleurs du mal, Leaves of Grass*, and a collected unpublished poems.

So the obsessions of modern poetry began with three revolutionaries, one Frenchman and two Americans. And poetry has happily not recovered from their original powers, and they have not faded. Of the three, Baudelaire is the most curious in that, while his attacks on conventional morality are unrelenting and his spleen and metaphysics made him a contemporary of Franz Kafka or a choice postmodern, his verse forms are relatively conventional—and, for the most part, magnificently successful. By contrast, Whitman and Dickinson tossed traditional forms out. Whitman's wandering free verse (from which poets in English from Eliot to Ginsberg derive) and Dickinson's profound, idiolectical obscurities of sense and syntax and her daring off-rhymes gave the twentieth century its poetic speech.

How could Baudelaire be at once traditional in form and icono-clastic in mind? The poet of the city and the urban poor, the angel of the damned and the underworld, the metaphysician in the gulf of nothingness (with a hint of light in interior nothingness) achieved poignancy and beauty within the borders of contemporary prosody. Regarding his formal verse, Anna Balakian says of his lesbian poems that he "wrote the most meticulously proper alexandrine to hide his heresies." At the same time she shrewdly observes that his yoking of conventional form to radical sense is "perhaps the most perfect example of the innovative poetics of Baudelaire."[1] Though more radical and subversive in theme than his contemporaries, he followed the sonorous verse of Victor Hugo, and went back to François Villon and Pierre de Ronsard for more substantial inspiration for his dissent and song.

Baudelaire's achievement is all the more astonishing when he is compared to the canonized French romantics, his contemporaries, who happened, following the habit of the age, to use traditional forms. Their lot is not a happy one. The verse of Vigny, Lamartine, Hugo, and Gautier scarcely speaks to us today, and the poets are little read outside of the classroom. The older poets could not, as Baudelaire did, go beyond the formulaic thought and tropes of their time. But Baudelaire remains essential. His alchemy of traditional music and revolution startled his generation as it moves ours.

It must also be said that Baudelaire's explosive mixture of dis-senting message in traditional form has remained exuberantly alive in the work of other major poets throughout the twentieth century. After the first decade, old poesy disappeared, but not the classical forms. Among world poets, many radical modernist poets sang their message in traditional forms. Federico García Lorca, Jorge Guillén, Jorge Luis Borges, Vladimir Mayakovsky, Osip Mandel-stam, Marina Tsvetayeva, and W. H. Auden were for the most part strict formalists. Indeed, in our increasingly eclectic period, the battles between traditional form and free verse are just about over.

How can we compare Baudelaire and the voice in his poems? There is always some correspondence between the artist's life and the work. In Baudelaire's case, while the poet took every freedom to invent, imagine, dream, and delude, to wear masks and assume poetic disguises, there remains an interchangeability between the persona created in the poems and the debt-ridden poet who changed apartments to flee creditors, who knew the sub rosa streets of prostitutes, thieves, beggars, and gamblers, his companions in life and verse, and who was forever dedicated to loving a woman. The woman's name changed, but the experience is inevitably ecstatic and devastating. Baudelaire the hounded man in the streets of Paris and Baudelaire the speaker in *Les Fleurs du mal* constitute a single, cumulative voice. He is the sickly fated lover of the beautiful and the exotic outcast. He is damnation and salvation. He is the misfit with fellow city misfits. Despite Baudelaire's guises of persona and critical dicta of artifice and artificiality, of artistic freedom from the self, in no poet with whom I am familiar is there a more constant correlation between the person and the poem.

Baudelaire looks outward to detail failures and degradations in city or country refuge, and looks inward to record broken spirits and extinguished soul light. No interesting life is easy or without profound pain, and Baudelaire's harrowing life was also his poetic treasure chest of experience. He used many conventional symbols of literature, including classical and neoclassical ones, but his primary source was his own mirror, in which he saw and converted the rawness of his existence into a singular art. In his erotic, even sadistic musings about the love object, in base despair, and in remote paradises he descends into nothingness to find something new. The poet of France sang his truths and aesthetic lies as long as his dandy youth, disappointed manhood, and dying syphilitic body gave him life.

How does Baudelaire do it? Wherein the alchemy? His subjects are luridly fascinating, filled with essential pathos and glimpses of colorfully tropical and Parisian transcendence, and the formal music in most of his poems is insuperable. But these descriptions of means and subjects do not explain his genius. Nor does Baudelaire's persistence as the major poet of his language depend on the dubious categories in which he is framed—the first symbolist, the first modernist, the first great decadent poet of the nineteenth century. I think the reasons that Baudelaire's poems work are rudimentary. The poems give pleasure, they inform, they sing, and they profoundly move us. Once exposed to them, we are purged and altered forever.

Charles Baudelaire, taking his external cue from tradition, made his sonnets and quatrains into his life book and bible. He is king of a rainy kingdom or companion to thin Parisian prostitutes keeping warm by clutching sticks of fire to their breasts; and in each depiction of person, cityscape, spleen, and sorrowful soul he is magical and right. The poems work through reading after reading. He is the master poet, by artifice and inspiration, by sonority and acute image, and we are crushed with dark emotion.

Charles-Pierre Baudelaire was born on April 9, 1821, in Paris. As with many poets, the circumstances of his childhood were to be the source of both his character and his writing for the rest of his life. Baudelaire's idyllic first years with his beloved father François, who was sixty-two when he married twenty-eight-year-old Caroline Archenbaut Defayis, were altered with his father's death in 1827, just six years later. The father displayed great affection for the boy, and is said to have left his elegant eighteenth-century manners to the young adoring Charles. Charles the later dandy, who was unusually courteous, often under extreme duress and even rage, was in many ways following dutifully the decorum of his dead father. Another idyllic year passed with his mother, whom he adored and to whom he was attached all his life in a hate/love bondage. Many years after his father's death, he recalls the little house they rented at Neuilly (3, rue de la Seine):

> I still recall our little house, out there
> Beyond the town, white-painted, with its air
> Of calm; . . . [2]

Then, twenty months later, in November 1827, like Hamlet's mother she betrayed him by marrying Major Jacques Aupick, a shining career officer who would become a general and ambassador to Turkey. Aupick, forty at the time of his marriage, provided comfort and security to the young widow. In the first years, Baudelaire's hostility to his stepfather was muted. When in 1832 the family moved to Lyon, where Aupick was stationed, Charles was immediately sent to a boarding school, the Collège Royal. It was a dark exile. The school, with its gloomy structures, somber vaults, and dank chapel in a town heavy with coal fumes that often hid the sun, was not lost on the poet. The bleak setting, which Baudelaire called "calamity itself," was to enter his mature poems of city life. Always an avid student of architecture, as he was of painting and sculpture, the poet later recalled the chapel's "variegated marbles" and its "monstrous Jesuitical style."[3]

His stepfather was soon promoted to colonel and in 1836 was assigned to Paris, where he was Chief of the First Division's General Staff. Charles became a boarder at the Lycée Louis-le-Grand, another gloomy structure. There he seriously began his lifelong study of literature and the arts. He read French as well as Greek and Latin, and won first prize three years in a row for poems he wrote in Latin. Then, in his last year, in 1849 when he was almost eighteen, he was expelled from Louis-le-Grand for an incident in class. A friend had slipped him a note, and he swallowed it rather than give it up and divulge the name of the giver. This act of courage or misfortune became a significant event in his life. As a result of his expulsion, he was sent to the Ecole des Chartes, a preparatory school for the baccalauréat examinations, which he was to pass. At this time he met the writers Gustave Le Vavasseur, Sainte-Beuve, and Théophile Gautier. Also in 1849, he announced to his parents, much to their consternation, that he would become a writer. In the following year we find him enrolled in the university to study law, but he apparently never attended classes. By now Baudelaire, barely eighteen, had plunged into the bohemian life of the Latin Quarter.

The young poet was the impeccably dressed dandy, often, as seen in photographs, in black. But despite his fastidious appearance ("dressed as neatly as a secretary at the British embassy" according to Le Vavasseur),[4] he had by then broken in fundamental ways with his bourgeois background. Even in boarding school, he wrote Sainte-Beuve, he had known "pernicious evenings" and "restless nights" dedicated to the flesh. That he spoke of "yielding to his temptations" reveals that the experiences were intensified with feelings of guilt, which his Catholic schooling only enforced. All these conflicting messages—of religion, art, social compassion, debauchery—served to dramatize the "flowers of evil," the epithet he used appropriately to sum up his poems. Soon he found a mistress, Sarah, who was a squint-eyed, ugly, and impoverished prostitute, all of which apparently attracted him. Because of her strange eyes, he called her la Louchette. Baudelaire was loyal to her long after they had ceased to be lovers. But from Sarah he contracted syphilis, which was to hasten his death. He had begun what he was to call his "life damned from the beginning."[5]

The Paris *quartiers* were not only evening adventures. Baudelaire spent his days at libraries, in museums, in galleries, and especially with other literary friends. On February 25, 1840, at the age of nineteen, he wrote a long letter to Victor Hugo, who was to be his helpful and compassionate friend through all the last years of his life when, after 1848, Hugo himself was in political exile in Belgium. In it he expressed his admiration, an urgent request for an answer, and, surprisingly, the modest apology: "All this is not well expressed— I think better than I write. But I hope that as you too have been young you'll guess what I leave unspoken."[6] And he had already established friendships with the poet Gérard de Nerval and the novelist Honoré de Balzac. After his first meeting with Balzac, he related the event to his friend the poet Le Vavasseur, who tells us: "Balzac and Baudelaire were walking in opposite directions on one of the quais of the Left Bank. Baudelaire stopped in front of Balzac and began laughing as if he had known him for ten years. Balzac stopped in his turn and replied with a resounding laugh, as if he had found a long-lost friend. And after having *recognized* each other at a glance and with a greeting, there they were, walking and talking in mutual rapture, incapable of astonishing each other."[7]

The poet's literary conquests did not calm M. and Mme Aupick's anxiety about their son's waywardness, and so they took five thousand francs from Charles's inheritance and sent him on the ship *Paquebot-des-Mers-du-Sud* to India. They wished to snatch him from "the perdition in the streets of Paris" and hoped that somehow the voyage would change his ways. At the same time, as Claude Pichois points out, Aupick told Charles that if indeed he were to be a poet he should have something to write about, which the trip would provide.[8] This casts Aupick in a slightly more favorable light. The ship sailed from Bordeaux for the Cape of Good Hope and the subcontinent. The trip was not without its own adventures. In a typhoon off the Cape, the ship's masts broke and the vessel almost sank. Baudelaire worked with the crew to raise a tarpaulin against what was left of the guy-ropes, and they managed to right the ship again. All this is recorded in the captain's log. Charles was a well-mannered passenger but extremely lonely and homesick among the businessmen and military officers, who had no interest in literature or in engaging in conversations with the young, strange poet. After nine months, before reaching Calcutta, he decided to go home. The ship stopped at Mauritius Island for repairs and then backtracked to Reunion Island, where Baudelaire waited for another ship to return him to France. Although he was unhappy and at the time seemed unwilling to appreciate the startling landscapes and exotic people, the trip supplied him with images of paradise, sea voyage, and colorful dreams that provided balance for the bleakness of his Paris haunts. Several of his poems were probably written on Reunion Island, where he stayed for forty-five days, and his essential symbol representing the isolated poet, the albatross, derives from the killing of an albatross that he witnessed on the crossing:

> Often will sailors, for their sport, ensnare
> The albatross, flying with languid sweep—
> Sea-bird companion, soaring on the air—
> Behind their boats, plying the bitter deep.

Then, as in a medieval bestiary, the poem concludes with the moral explanation. Like the albatross, who is free in spirit high in the sky, the poet, once caught on the land below, hobbles in exile from transcendence:

> So too the Poet, like that prince of space
> Who haunts the storm and scorns the archer's bow:

Mocked, jeered, his giant's wings hobble his pace
When exiled from his heights to earth below.[9]

Soon after his return to Paris, Charles, unreformed, unrepentant, joined his literary coterie again and pursued his night life at the Hashish Club, where he would meet Gautier, or in the company of his new mistress, Jeanne Duval, a quadroon whom Baudelaire's mother called his "Black Venus." Jeanne Duval was the singular woman of Baudelaire's life and poems. The others were by comparison insignificant. For his parents this new misadventure was intolerable. Their hold on him was moral and financial, but in April 1842 he reached his majority and, with his mother and stepfather, made arrangements for his father's inheritance to be turned over to him. For the moment he was free of their purse strings. The general and his mother feared he would mismanage the fund, which in the first years he did with disastrous haste. They themselves, however, had not been generous in drawing up the settlement. They deducted some 34,000 francs, a substantial hunk of the inheritance, to compensate them for having provided their son with room, board, and education. It left him with 100,000 francs, invested safely, which, if he lived modestly, should provide him enough to live on without diminishing the principle.

Baudelaire took a small apartment on L'Ile Saint-Louis in the Seine, and furnished it with paintings and furniture that he bought from an unscrupulous dealer named Arondel. He signed promissory notes, and at the time of his death he was still paying off debts. The poet also set up Jeanne Duval in a small apartment, which he furnished with oriental rugs and hangings. Duval was an actress in a small Latin Quarter theater. Her grandmother had been sold into slavery in Guinea and placed in a brothel in France. Her mother, it is thought, was also a prostitute. Duval is described by the photographer Nadar as having "a small, delicate nose with exquisitely chiseled nostrils, and a mouth that appeared Egyptian... with an admirable set of teeth between strong, beautifully sculptured lips. Her whole air was grave, proud, even a little disdainful. From the narrow waist up, her body was long, sinuous like an adder, and particularly remarkable for the exuberant, unbelievable development of her bust, which gave her the appearance of a branch bowed under the burden of its fruit."[10] The poet called her "his sole diversion, his only pleasure, and his unique friend."[11] Although their relationship was stormy, and biographers have treated her as Baudelaire's bad angel, he remained devoted to her even after the first five years, after which they drew apart. At the time of Baudelaire's last sickness, he was desolate that he could not help her financially.

Charles's liaison with Jeanne and his intemperate spending alarmed his parents—in two years much of his trust fund was gone—and Madame Aupick decided in 1844 to appoint the lawyer Ancelle as legal guardian for her son's finances. Charles would be allotted a small monthly allowance. He was humiliated, furious, and later claimed that this deed had ruined his life; at the time he saw it as confirming another failure. In the last years of his life, however, he reconciled with Ancelle, and the two men grew fond of each other. Meanwhile, the poet raged, and in June 1845 he made a somewhat unconvincing attempt at suicide by stabbing himself lightly with a knife. In his suicide letter he asked Ancelle to look after Jeanne.

Baudelaire had been publishing poems for his future volume, but without great notice. He was hesitant about bringing out his collection, and for years he kept changing its focus. As the title *Flowers of Evil* implies,[12] he was obsessed with the notion of evil, and to accept or reject it he had first to express it. After 1861 he declared that he was a Catholic and that *Les Fleurs du mal* was grounded in Catholic ideas. But apart from evil and religion, though never free of them, the poems speak beauty and escape, love and death, and an overriding metaphysic. And the mood of melancholy morality may at once be infused with an ecstasy of otherness and joy when the poet, for a moment, climbs high or descends so low as to find light. In poems where corruption and beauty seem inseparable, the poems give off both light and darkness.

The book was dedicated to Théophile Gautier. It was a strange dedication to a friend whose doctrine of art for art's sake, of "enamels" and "cameos," was so much at odds with Baudelaire's own intense morality—or, according to how the poems were received, intensely sensual immorality. *Les Fleurs du mal,* published by his faithful friend Poulet-Malassis, went on sale on June 25, 1857. But it was not well received. In July, a crushing review in *Le Figaro* condemned the book as "the putrescence of the human heart." Baudelaire's close friend Sainte-Beuve by now carried great weight as a critic. The poet begged him to review *Les Fleurs*—in private the critic was known to have praised the book—but Sainte-Beuve failed him, as he always would. Also in July the book was publicly denounced as offending public morality, which led to the prosecution of Baudelaire and Poulet-Malassis. Author and publisher were dragged to court, convicted, and fined heavily, and six of the poems were banned from the book. Only an appeal to the empress Eugénie resulted in a reduction of the fines.

Here we see the poet at thirty-six, having just published the most important volume of poetry ever printed in the French language. He is at the summit of his literary and critical talents. He is also at the nadir of his many painful failures. Public recognition of his controversial volume is negative. The poet's legal and financial affairs are in terrible shape, and his health is fatally impaired. What carries him is art, his art, and his good writer and painter companions. Among the painters he will maintain loyal and intimate friendships with Courbet and Manet. He often accompanies Manet to the Tuileries, where the painter does his open air studies. And of course what sustains him is also his difficult attachment to the women of his life, including his mother, Caroline Aupick. Two months before the publication of *Les Fleurs du mal,* General Aupick died. From then on, Charles and his mother carry on an an uneasy relationship through letters and visits. But for now, after the catastrophic reception of *Les Fleurs* in Paris, Baudelaire sets to work to revise and enlarge his collection, which he will republish in 1861. The poem is always there.

The second edition of *Les Fleurs du mal,* in 1861, contained 126 poems, of which 35 were new pieces. Encouraged by the publication and desperately in debt, Baudelaire conceived the notion of being elected to the French Academy and wrote to the secretary, declaring his candidacy. Only Alfred de Vigny, who was dying of cancer, believed in Baudelaire's genius and would have him be an

"Academician," but he knew it was not possible to obtain the vote. He advised him to withdraw his candidacy. Baudelaire accepted the humiliation and withdrew. By now, his sicknesses were overcoming him by day and especially by night. That terrible line in the *Intimate Journals* of January 1862, "I felt passing over me the wind of the wing of madness," tells the horror.

Charles Baudelaire was condemned to hope forever. He was also condemned to carry a chimera of despair. He pinned his last hope of fame, decent publication, and money on a lecture series he would give in Brussels. On April 24, 1863, he left Paris for Belgium. Nothing worked out. He did become a frequent guest at the home of his friend Victor Hugo, who was living his exile in Brussels. And some good literary words came to him from France. Sainte-Beuve told him of the enthusiasm for him of two young poets, Paul Verlaine and Stéphane Mallarmé, for his work, adding that if Baudelaire were in Paris he would become "an authority, an oracle, a consultant poet."[13] As usual, there was a patronizing overtone to Sainte-Beuve's praise, but he did send him Verlaine's and Mallarmé's publications. In *L'Artiste*, February 1, 1865, Mallarmé wrote, "In winter, when I'm tired of my torpor, I plunge with delight into the cherished pages of *Les Fleurs du mal*. No sooner is my Baudelaire open than I am drawn into a surprising landscape, which lives in my eye with the intensity of those created by profound opium."

The poet gave five prearranged lectures in May and June, the first on Delacroix, which was very well received and reviewed. The second was on Gautier. Baudelaire was happy and confident, but his very first words were a mischievous and unduly modest comment on how this second lecture might lack the innocent freshness of the first: "This is the second time I have spoken in public, and it was in front of you, at my first lecture, that I lost what might be called my virginity as a speaker, which is no more to be regretted than the other."[14] The women in charge of young ladies from a local boarding school rose in indignation and soon there was scarcely anyone left in the hall. We have a precise description of that event from a young writer and admirer of *Les Fleurs du mal*, Camille Lemonnier, who had slipped into the room toward the end of the talk. Thirty years later in his memoir *La Vie belge* he recalled: "His pale, clean-shaven face could be discerned in semidarkness about the shade of the lamp; I could see his eyes moving like black suns; his mouth seemed to live with a life of its own, separate from the animation and expressiveness of his face; the thin lips quivered, like a taught violin-string under the bow of the words he spoke, and the whole head rose like a tower, dominating the attentive but bewildered audience."[15] The poet continued lecturing, the hall now empty except for Lemonnier, as if nothing had happened. He ended his talk on Gautier, saying, "I salute Théophile Gautier as my master, the great poet of the century." He gave three stiff little bows as if he were standing before a real audience, and left.

The last three lectures were likewise a disappointment, or, according to the memoirs of a young journalist, Georges Barral, who covered them, "a disaster."

After the lectures, to the astonishment of his friends, Baudelaire stayed on in Brussels. He was safe from his creditors but had little to live on. And he couldn't settle his hotel bill at the Hôtel du Grand Miroir, where he lived in a small cell of a room. Since the room had no clock on the mantelpiece and his watch was at the pawn shop, he told time by the church bells. However, he did have visitors, and despite everything he was treated with the dignity of an important writer, not only by a few friends such as Hugo and the photographer Charles Neyt but also by occasional visitors such as his photographer friend Nadar, who was in Brussels to ascend in his new balloon, *Le Géant*.

In February of 1885, Baudelaire suffered a mild stroke. Soon after, he recovered enough to rush back to Paris with the hope of borrowing money. He saw his mother in Honfleur, and she herself borrowed money to pay his most pressing debts. In Paris again, exhausted, while examining a catafalque in the Jesuit church of Saint-Loup, he had another, more severe attack. He returned to Brussels, where he had a major stroke and lost his ability to speak. He could utter only one word, and it happened to be a curse. After staying in a nursing home for a few months, he was sent back to the clinic Emile Duval in Paris. In January 1867, his publisher wanted to bring out a new edition of *Les Fleurs du mal* with the twenty-six new poems that would eventually become part of the collection, but, through gestures, Baudelaire indicated that he could not agree to it until he was well enough to correct the proofs. He did not recover and remained, as he had been these last years in Belgium, profoundly despondent, his mind clear but elsewhere.

On August 31, 1867, Charles Baudelaire died in his mother's arms. The funeral took place on September 2. There were many speeches. As his body was lowered into the Cimetière Montparnasse, there was a sudden clap of thunder and the wind blew a shower of yellow leaves down onto the coffin. It began to pour with rain, and everyone ran for shelter.

Baudelaire was soon famous, not only in France but everywhere. His complete works were quickly published by Michel Lévy. His mother, now persuaded of his distinction, spent the last four years of her life doing everything to ensure that her son would not be forgotten as a great poet.

In Baudelaire there is great soul. And in his life that soul (meaning "spirit" or "consciousness," not a divine entity) held the hopes and the miseries of the artist. There was room in that soul for very little else, other than his good friendships, his disastrous but spirit-feeding loves, and his vision of the poor in the city of Paris. And what was in him came out on paper. What he wrote also fed his soul, so that he could go on to the next poem. Soul and poem married. Both person and art joined in an ecstasy of escape and transcendence in which the person, unwilling to conform to a dutiful middle-class life, became his other, the persona in the poems. Being other, being elsewhere, as the word ecstasy means, he plunged physically, spiritually, and artistically into the degradations, suffering, and consummations that his embattled years permitted him.

Rainer Maria Rilke ended his sonnet "Archaic Torso of Apollo": *Du musst dein Leben ändern* ("You must change your life"). It is not easy to do that. Baudelaire could not do it. But Baudelaire does change us. We are not the same after knowing him well. This man and writer who hid behind so much artifice is the most candid of poets. If there is misery and beauty in the world, if there is light in the *néant*, in nothingness, his poems cannot affect any of these phenomena—but he reveals them. His poems are a glass. And he permits us vision to feel.

The fidelity of the translator to Baudelaire is determined by one criterion: the poem must work in English with all the force, meaning, and formal beauty of the original. It must work in *sound* as well as denotation. If the poem's music is ignored, the reader should put the translation down. The translator must know that the larger connotative meaning of the poem includes its music and demands in translation an equally resonant poem.

How has Shapiro handled the music? I should first note that there have been two essential ways of rendering Baudelaire into English: those that ignore and those that recreate Baudelaire's formal music—which in the original is constant and essential. In the best of the translations that ignore the formal music, the poems may read well in English. But, as in the translations of Baudelaire's contemporary, Constantine Cavafy, the reader has no clue that Baudelaire worked his rhyme and meter into invisible forms, and that through enjambment and subtle metrical inversions his music is never singsong metronymic but wondrously overheard. Curiously, those translations that ignore musical prosody also take extreme freedom with the literal meaning, as if needing to redeem the poem from its original formal, yet innovative, music and its nineteenth-century rhetoric. Baudelaire sang and moves us. In the nonformal translations, Baudelaire talks quite nicely as a twentieth-century poet. But his verse will lack the conviction of song.

The second way is to let Baudelaire sing. There are as many dangers, perhaps more, in carrying over the music. Normally, it is done poorly, and we have padding or jingjang. One must have the inspired skills of the source poet, at least at the moment of translating, to recreate in English. One is a poet in the act of translating, and nothing less will give us a great translation. And the difficulties of form are not obstacles. The difficulties both save us from being seduced by the obvious literal surface and provoke the imagination to come up with ten or twenty solutions. One of these essential solutions will—it has been my experience—*click* and bring through not only the music but also a closer denotative meaning than an obvious literal gloss. So sound and statement magnify each other. Then, and only then, is one faithful to the multiple semantic and esthetic qualities of the poem. Only then is a new poem born.

Norman Shapiro has chosen to let Baudelaire sing. And to do so he has recreated in English the despondent resonance of the dark Baudelaire and the tawdry realism of city figures—the blind, the drunk, the depraved—each a parable of survival. And he has also painted the candid, fantastic, and bejeweled sensuality of erotic love, the poet's metaphysical plunges and sage resignation, and the ecstatic pictures in paradisal passages. Shapiro has not padded, he has not contorted English, and he has remained close to sound and letter. His work is an invisible magic. And, rare among contemporary poets who have translated, he has not stolen Baudelaire's voice and replaced it with his own. When Robert Fitzgerald, the translator of Homer, went to see Ezra Pound in Saint Elizabeth's hospital in Washington D.C., he asked Pound how he should do Homer. Uncharacteristically and at odds with his own practice, Pound answered, "Let Homer speak."

Shapiro has let Baudelaire speak, sing, and meditate in the poem. His translations are poems, and they are also Baudelaire's resonant voice in English.

WILLIS BARNSTONE

NOTES

In addition to the works cited below, I have drawn from Lois Hyslop, *Charles Baudelaire Revisited* (New York: Twayne, 1992); and Pascal Pia, *Baudelaire*, trans. Patrick Gregory (New York: Grove Press, 1961).

1. Anna Balakian, Introduction, in Charles Baudelaire, *The Flowers of Evil and Paris Spleen*, trans. William H. Crosby (Brockport, NY: BOA Editions, 1991), 9.

2. See below, 165.

3. M. A. Ruff, *Baudelaire*, trans. and slightly abridged by Agnes Kertsz (New York: New York University Press, 1966), 6.

4. Cited in Ruff, *Baudelaire*.

5. Letter to his mother, December 4, 1854, cited in Pia, *Baudelaire*, 21.

6. *Selected Letters of Charles Baudelaire*, ed. and trans. Rosemary Lloyd (Chicago: University of Chicago Press, 1986), 20.

7. Cited in Ruff, *Baudelaire*, 16.

8. Claude Pichois, *Baudelaire,* trans. Graham Robb (London: Hamish Hamilton, 1987), 69.

9. See below, 9.

10. F. T. Nader, *Charles Baudelaire intime: Le poète vierge* (Paris, 1911); translation of this passage is drawn from F. W. J. Hemmings, *The Poet Damned: A Biography* (New York: Scribners, 1982), 7–8.

11. Cited in Ruff, *Baudelaire,* 31.

12. The title was not Baudelaire's first choice but was provided by a friend. I owe this information and much more to my colleague Rosemary Lloyd, who carefully read these pages.

13. Letter of December 13, 1865, in Pichois, *Baudelaire,* 334.

14. Cited in Enid Starkie, *Charles Baudelaire* (London: Faber & Faber, 1946), 471.

15. Cited in Hemmings, *The Poet Damned,* 205.

Preface

Whether we think of him as "the father of modern poetry," as he is
sometimes called, or as the last of the Romantics, Charles Baude-
laire cuts a majestic figure in the history of western literature.
Grotesque, to be sure, but no less majestic in that grotesqueness.
Morose and melancholic, unfettered in his guilt-ridden glorification
of sensual excesses, he seems, on the one hand, to announce the
melodic vaguenesses of the Symbolists, and, on the other, to echo
the angst and self-pity of his Romantic elders, along with all their
respect for traditional poetic form. And if the "obscenities" that
scandalized his straitlaced contemporaries and that brought down
the wrath of the law upon his head, and upon his work, have long
since paled in the moral and lexical anarchy of later generations, he
remains nonetheless a prototype: a poetic incarnation of the spirit
of Evil; and that, thanks to a relatively meager bouquet of "flowers"
that bloomed from the soil of his perverse and troubled genius.

That said, anyone who knows my other incursions into the trans-
lation of French literature may wonder why I have ventured here,
of all places. What is a translator of French farce and fable—of a
robustly comic Feydeau and a moral, often lighthearted La Fon-
taine—doing amid the miasmic depths and pervasive demonic
gloom of Baudelairean passion? ("Passion," that is, in both its
senses: suffering as well as lust.) For those tempted to ask, the
answer is quite straightforward. For me, the joy of translation
lies in the challenge the text presents.

Now, as every fellow translator will admit, translating any
poetry is challenging per se; especially if one wants to get right
what Seamus Heaney has called "the tune" and "the tone," the mes-
sage and the manner, neither of which is really completely satisfac-
tory without the other. Baudelaire's poetry is more so than most.
Any translator thirsting for challenge will certainly find it here: the
double challenge of bringing across his disquieting "tune" into an
English capable of the highs and the lows of his French lexicon,
and of doing so in a form—metered and rhymed, and most of the

time cast in the venerable sonnet mold—that helps present in our language the "tone" his work resonates with in his. To translate Baudelaire's ideas and feelings is often demanding enough; to do so without sacrificing the elements of style, sound, mood, and in a structured verse to which he himself was obviously partial, is supremely so. Witness, indeed, the results of the many translators who have accosted *Les Fleurs du mal* in the past, in whole or in part. To my taste, at least, and with all the objectivity one translator can muster for others' renderings, they vary widely in quality, from the tepidly inept to the artistically and aesthetically compelling. Most, however, fall variously in between: some, elegant exercises in idiosyncratic paraphrase; others, intentional attempts to turn Baudelaire into a formless twentieth-century free-versifier; some, hewing closely to his formal constraints, but often contrived and tortured in the process; others, endeavoring to echo the richness of his music, but forced to resort to wan assonances, almost-rhymes, and graceless, limping meters.

The inherent difficulties in translating Baudelaire likely would not have lured me, however, to put aside other lagging projects and accost him in turn, were it not for another, more specific, immediate challenge, one stemming, indeed, from the very multiplicity of others' attempts. The fact is, two years ago this collection was not even the glimmer of an idea. The catalyst for it appeared in the form of an invitation from Professor Carrol Coates to participate, several months later, at the 1996 convention of the American Literary Translators' Association, in a panel whose subject was to be "On Translating Baudelaire," and whose format would be a comparative study of various translators' versions of several of the poems from *Les Fleurs du mal*. "I know you've never translated any Baudelaire," colleague Coates observed, going on to explain that he thought my general experience in translating French verse would, nonetheless, make me a useful participant. Even as I was replying to the effect that I had actually thought now and then about giving Baudelaire a try, his observation had begun to assume the proportions of a gauntlet cast down at my feet. No, I hadn't translated any Baudelaire, true enough. But did that mean I couldn't? Well, to make a longish story short, I spent the next few weeks intent on proving to myself that I could, by working out versions of the half-dozen poems that were to serve as a basis for the panel's eventual discussion.

It could, of course, have ended respectably then and there. And it would have, were it not for the fact that translators are no less subject to obsessions and compulsions than any other members of the species. By the time I realized that mine were taking over, even at the expense of deadlines for other projects, I had done about a dozen. At that point, rather satisfied with my results, I began thinking that a small collection might be in order: perhaps twenty or so translations, elegantly presented with lots of illustrations, as a coffee-table art book of sorts. But compulsions don't release their hold on demand. As I mused from time to time on that publishing possibility I continued to let myself do "just one more... just one more.... " How could I, after all, not include this one—a favorite—or that one—a challenging one-of-a-kind example of Baudelairean virtuosity?

And the more I did, the more the work took on a momentum, almost a life of its own. Other translators will, I am sure, recognize the phenomenon. The "just one more"s began adding up, well past the projected "twenty or so," as I found myself getting into Baudelaire's skin, in a manner of speaking. Or at least into his mind. Some, of a spiritual persuasion, might be tempted to wax more metaphysical and suggest that he, rather, was getting into mine, ascribing what is merely a (harmless) psychological aberration, a kind of compulsive *furor scribendi*, to "the spirit of the author," at work somehow in an inspiratory capacity. Indeed, it would be comforting to think that our chosen authors are out there somewhere, disembodied entities—the dead ones, that is—establishing a mystical rapport with us and guiding our pens or our word processors in the posthumous re-creation of their art across linguistic divides. (In Baudelaire's case I would rather hope not: though I would happily host his talent, I would, frankly, want no part of the rest of his spirit!) And while I do believe that a translator, to re-create the "tune," must, as I say, identify for a time with the author's psyche, I know that no amount of "inspiration," otherworldly or otherwise, can take the place of a well-developed and meticulous, self-demanding craft. It is that craft, with all the labor that accompanies it, that helps the translator face the most difficult of challenges: that of making the whole thing look easy, unstrained, and utterly effortless.

At any rate, as my "twenty or so" grew gently into "thirty or so" and beyond, it became clear that my collection was taking on quite a different shape. The present seventy or so, about half of *Les Fleurs du mal,* are the result, with by far the largest number taken from "Spleen et Idéal," the major section of the work, but with the other five titled sections ("Tableaux parisiens," "Le Vin," "Fleurs du mal," "Révolte," and "La Mort") represented as well. Since it was never my intention to translate the entire collection, a choice had to be made. Mine was guided not only by personal taste— a criterion that, proverbially, brooks no discussion—but also by a desire to present Baudelaire in all his variety; a variety of subject and mood greater than one might expect, given his basic splenetic disposition, and especially of form. For, while the sonnet is clearly his favorite vehicle, it will be noticed that he (and, consequently, I) felt moved to maintain within its strict confines a considerable freedom of rhyme scheme and metric. Likewise his non-sonnets: free-ranging couplets, stanzaic verses of no fixed length, others of often capricious formal artistry—and all demanding to be transposed, according to my aesthetic lights at least, in corresponding manner, and with an ear for the no less challenging subtleties of his language and its music.

As luck would have it, I was unable to attend the ALTA conference and participate in the panel that had got this whole venture started. It was probably just as well. I am not sure that, after translating Baudelaire myself, my opinion of others' attempts could have been objective enough to be of much value. All that aside, I am grateful to Carrol Coates for unwittingly nudging me toward an undertaking that, with—and, indeed, because of—its challenges, has been a most gratifying one for me as translator. It will be even more so if I can feel that, on the one hand, readers with too little French to savor Baudelaire in the original can experience his art and craft through me, and that, on the other, those who do understand him can become more aware of all those challenges and appreciate at least one translator's way of coping with them.*

* * *

Second only to my late mother, whose poetic talents early inspired and continue to inspire me, my thanks go to Evelyn Singer Simha, to whom this work is gratefully dedicated. Her literary insights, aesthetic judgment, and personal devotion have, as ever, been unstinting and indispensable.

Many others have been generous with their moral, physical, and artistic support, or helpful with a variety of practical chores. To them all—Lillian Bulwa, Carla Chrisfield, Rita Dempsey, Rosalind Eastaway, Raphi Folsom, Sylvia and Allan Kliman, Robert and Jana Kiely, Vicki Macy, Jeffrey Mehlman, Mary Lou Nelles, Seymour O. Simches, Louisa Solano, Marc Talusan, and Caldwell Titcomb—my appreciation for the parts, large and small, that they all have played.

Very special thanks as well to Morris Philipson and Randolph Petilos of the University of Chicago Press, for their confidence; to Willis Barnstone, for his graceful prose and gracious judgments; and to colleague and illustrator David Schorr, for his constant encouragement no less than for his superb artistic talent.

And, of course, my hearty appreciation to Carrol Coates, godfather of this collection, without whose inspiration it would—to put it in properly Baudelairean terms—never have seen the dark of night.

NORMAN R. SHAPIRO

*The French text used for the present translations is that of the 1861 edition of *Les Fleurs du mal* as presented by Yves-G. Le Dantec in the series Bibliothèque de la Pléiade (Baudelaire, *Œuvres* [Paris: Gallimard, 1958]).

ILLUSTRATOR'S PREFACE

Many of my prints, drawings, and paintings—even those that are not illustrations—have a basis in text, and few texts have meant as much to me for as long as these poems of Baudelaire, in their various translations. A production of *Long Day's Journey into Night* at the Trinity Square Repertory Theater in Providence while I was in college sent me to the library to find the Arthur Symonds translation from which Jamie Tyrone, the older brother in the play, quotes in drunken reverie. Alongside it on the shelf I found another translation by Edna St. Vincent Millay, whose sonnets I was already outgrowing, and only through her Baudelaire did I understand the buried sexuality of her own poems.

Some years ago I did murals for a Toronto restaurant, Scaramouche, with characters from the Commedia dell'arte. In the bar I drew Pulcinella, the cynical hedonist, drinking himself to death on top of his own tomb. On the tomb I inscribed an epitaph, an English translation of Baudelaire's prose poem: "Be Always Drunken." I asked the client if I should include the original French as well, "After all," I said, "this is Canada!" But when he replied "Not to worry, most Torontonians aren't bilingual!" my response was to add a grand banner flying over Pulcinella's head emblazoned with the French.

Just over a decade ago I learned that a new translation of Baudelaire was about to be published and that an illustrator was being sought. I wanted the job, but they chose Michael Mazur, a printmaker/illustrator I have long valued as a friend and admired enormously as an artist. Life seldom offers second chances this specific; so when, last year, Norman Shapiro, whose translations from the whimsical to the bawdy I have illustrated before, told me that he was doing a Baudelaire with the University of Chicago Press and that they were hoping to illustrate it, I staged a campaign for the job, worthy of Gatsby for Daisy, or Domenichino for the dome of Sant'Andrea.

I explain to my printmaking students at Wesleyan that there are reasons other than repeatability to make prints. Each medium has its own nature: a woodcut looks like a woodcut and nothing else. I explain that the intaglio media (engraving, etching, aquatint, mezzotint, drypoint, all of which, as here, may be used in combination) are capable of deep, rich, layered blacks and a dark "timbre" that no other media can approach. So the mood of these poems, at once lugubrious and licentious, their time of day—night or early morning—even their history, the glare and shadow of gaslit Paris, suggested deep marks on copper printed in dense, rag-wiped black.

Many people helped with the production of these prints. I am grateful to editor Randy Petilos for *carte blanche* (or should I say *noire*) in letting me select which poems I would illustrate and in allowing me to go ahead both with my desire to produce engravings and to expand the original plan from ten to eighteen in order to create a better visual sequence. The administration and trustees of Wesleyan generously provided a grant to support models and materials. Ken Botnick, the former director of Penland School of Craft, and Dana Moore, the program director, generously offered a residency including a print shop, where much of the work was completed. My assistant at Penland, Loy McWhirter, was an untiring source of labor and inspiration. My models—David Brick, Bill Mulaine, Loy McWhirter, Bruce Greene, Christopher Robinson, Wendy Gimbel, and Anne McAden—provided the most fundamental help and inspiration, and they held still. Nona Hershey not only knows more about printmaking technique than anyone alive but also always returns my phone calls. As always, the staff at Wesleyan assisted in many ways: Gloria Augeri and Will McCarthy in the Art Department, David Boule and Tommy Castelli at the machine shop, John Elmore and Jean Shaw at the Center for the Arts, Kate Truax at the slide library, and Nell Gould my print shop manager.

Many friends in the artistic and intellectual communities in which I live and work helped in various ways. For their knowing eyes, perceptive criticism, and other support I am particularly grateful to Arthur Williams, Phyllis Rose, Laurent de Brunhoff, Nona Hershey, Mark and Natalie Schorr, Jeffrey Schiff, Gay Smith, Noah Isenberg, Tom Rapp, Douglas Sills, Andrew Szegedy-Maszak, Amy

Bernstein, Nina Felshin, Bob Trotman, Patrick Long, Marc Koplik, and Jeff Sarmiento.

There is no way I can find words in any language, original or translated, to thank Norman Shapiro, whom I now refer to as Gilbert, to my Sullivan—always with the reminder that Gilbert was the genius.

But it is to Mary Ryan, my dealer, and Catherine Ryan, who together do so much to allow me to be an artist, especially a printmaker, that I dedicate my work.

DAVID SCHORR

Selected Poems from *Les Fleurs du mal*

C'est le Diable qui tient les fils qui nous remuent!

Au Lecteur

La sottise, l'erreur, le péché, la lésine,
Occupent nos esprits et travaillent nos corps,
Et nous alimentons nos aimables remords,
Comme les mendiants nourrissent leur vermine.

Nos péchés sont têtus, nos repentirs sont lâches;
Nous nous faisons payer grassement nos aveux,
Et nous rentrons gaiement dans le chemin bourbeux,
Croyant par de vils pleurs laver toutes nos taches.

Sur l'oreiller du mal c'est Satan Trismégiste
Qui berce longuement notre esprit enchanté,
Et le riche métal de notre volonté
Est tout vaporisé par ce savant chimiste.

C'est le Diable qui tient les fils qui nous remuent!
Aux objets répugnants nous trouvons des appas;
Chaque jour vers l'Enfer nous descendons d'un pas,
Sans horreur, à travers des ténèbres qui puent.

Ainsi qu'un débauché pauvre qui baise et mange
Le sein martyrisé d'une antique catin,
Nous volons au passage un plaisir clandestin
Que nous pressons bien fort comme une vieille orange.

Serré, fourmillant, comme un million d'helminthes,
Dans nos cerveaux ribote un peuple de Démons,
Et, quand nous respirons, la Mort dans nos poumons
Descend, fleuve invisible, avec de sourdes plaintes.

Si le viol, le poison, le poignard, l'incendie,
N'ont pas encor brodé de leurs plaisants dessins
Le canevas banal de nos piteux destins,
C'est que notre âme, hélas! n'est pas assez hardie.

To the Reader

Folly, depravity, greed, mortal sin
Invade our souls and rack our flesh; we feed
Our gentle guilt, gracious regrets, that breed
Like vermin glutting on foul beggars' skin.

Our sins are stubborn; our repentance, faint.
We take a handsome price for our confession,
Happy once more to wallow in transgression,
Thinking vile tears will cleanse us of all taint.

On evil's cushion poised, His Majesty,
Satan Thrice-Great, lulls our charmed soul, until
He turns to vapor what was once our will:
Rich ore, transmuted by his alchemy.

He holds the strings that move us, limb by limb!
We yield, enthralled, to things repugnant, base;
Each day, toward Hell, with slow, unhurried pace,
We sink, uncowed, through shadows, stinking, grim.

Like some lewd rake with his old worn-out whore,
Nibbling her suffering teats, we seize our sly
Delight, that, like an orange—withered, dry—
We squeeze and press for juice that is no more.

Our brains teem with a race of Fiends, who frolic
Thick as a million gut-worms; with each breath,
Our lungs drink deep, suck down a stream of Death—
Dim-lit—to low-moaned whimpers melancholic.

If poison, fire, blade, rape do not succeed
In sewing on that dull embroidery
Of our pathetic lives their artistry,
It's that our soul, alas, shrinks from the deed.

Mais parmi les chacals, les panthères, les lices,
Les singes, les scorpions, les vautours, les serpents,
Les monstres glapissants, hurlants, grognants, rampants,
Dans la ménagerie infâme de vos vices,

Il en est un plus laid, plus méchant, plus immonde!
Quoiqu'il ne pousse ni grands gestes ni grand cris,
Il ferait volontiers de la terre un débris
Et dans un bâillement avalerait le monde;

C'est l'Ennui!—l'œil chargé d'un pleur involontaire,
Il rêve d'échafauds en fumant son houka.
Tu le connais, lecteur, ce monstre délicat,
—Hypocrite lecteur,—mon semblable,—mon frère!

And yet, among the beasts and creatures all—
Panther, snake, scorpion, jackal, ape, hound, hawk—
Monsters that crawl, and shriek, and grunt, and squawk,
In our vice-filled menagerie's caterwaul,

One worse is there, fit to heap scorn upon—
More ugly, rank! Though noiseless, calm, and still,
Yet would he turn the earth to scraps and swill,
Swallow it whole in one great, gaping yawn:

Ennui! That monster frail!—With eye wherein
A chance tear gleams, he dreams of gibbets, while
Smoking his hookah, with a dainty smile...
—You know him, reader,—hypocrite,—my twin!

L'Albatros

Souvent, pour s'amuser, les hommes d'équipage
Prennent des albatros, vastes oiseaux des mers,
Qui suivent, indolents compagnons de voyage,
La navire glissant sur les gouffres amers.

A peine les ont-ils déposés sur les planches,
Que ces rois de l'azur, maladroits et honteux,
Laissent piteusement leurs grandes ailes blanches
Comme des avirons traîner à côté d'eux.

Ce voyageur ailé, comme il est gauche et veule!
Lui, naguère si beau, qu'il est comique et laid!
L'un agace son bec avec un brûle-gueule,
L'autre mime, en boitant, l'infirme qui volait!

Le Poëte est semblable au prince des nuées
Qui hante la tempête et se rit de l'archer;
Exilé sur le sol au milieu des huées,
Ses ailes de géant l'empêchent de marcher.

The Albatross

Often will sailors, for their sport, ensnare
The albatross, flying with languid sweep—
Sea-bird companion, soaring on the air—
Behind their boats, plying the bitter deep.

Scarce are they thrust on deck than these proud kings
Of azure climes, awkward and mortified,
Let droop, pathetically, their vast white wings,
Like two oars, trailing useless by their side.

How clumsy this winged voyager! How weak,
Comic, and ugly! He, so fair of late!
Some, with their clay pipes, taunt him, jab his beak;
Some ape the erstwhile flier's limping gait.

So too the Poet, like that prince of space,
Who haunts the storm and scorns the archer's bow:
Mocked, jeered, his giant's wings hobble his pace
When exiled from his heights to earth below.

9

Elévation

Au-dessus des étangs, au-dessus des vallées,
Des montagnes, des bois, des nuages, des mers,
Par delà le soleil, par delà les éthers,
Par delà les confins des sphères étoilées,

Mon esprit, tu te meus avec agilité,
Et, comme un bon nageur qui se pâme dans l'onde,
Tu sillonnes gaiement l'immensité profonde
Avec une indicible et mâle volupté.

Envole-toi bien loin de ces miasmes morbides;
Va te purifier dans l'air supérieur,
Et bois, comme une pure et divine liqueur,
Le feu clair qui remplit les espaces limpides.

Derrière les ennuis et les vastes chagrins
Qui chargent de leur poids l'existence brumeuse,
Heureux celui qui peut d'une aile vigoureuse
S'élancer vers les champs lumineux et sereins!

Celui dont les pensers, comme des alouettes,
Vers les cieux le matin prennent un libre essor,
—Qui plane sur la vie, et comprend sans effort
Le langage des fleurs et des choses muettes!

Elevation

High above valley, mountain, wood, and pond,
Above the seas, the clouds, the ether vast;
Out past the sun itself, the stars; out past
The very limits of the great Beyond,

O spirit mine! You move with grace among
Those deeps; as swimmers might, a-swoon, who trace
A wake of manly bliss, cleaving apace
The waves, with pleasure that defies the tongue.

Fly! Flee these putrid wastes! Let yourself be
Washed pure, cleansed, soaring higher, and ever higher;
Drink of that heavenly liquor, that bright fire
That fills the realms of limpid purity.

Happy the man—despite the frets, despite
The woes that smother life's dim murkiness—
Who, strong of purpose, flies high, nonetheless,
Off to the calm and peaceful fields of light;

Whose thoughts, in morning flight on lark-like wings,
Rise to the heavens, above the fray, swept free;
—Who understands, aloft, effortlessly,
The speech of flowers and of all silent things!

Correspondances

La Nature est un temple où de vivants piliers
Laissent parfois sortir de confuses paroles;
L'homme y passe à travers des forêts de symboles
Qui l'observent avec des regards familiers.

Comme de longs échos qui de loin se confondent
Dans une ténébreuse et profonde unité,
Vaste comme la nuit et comme la clarté,
Les parfums, les couleurs et les sons se répondent.

Il est des parfums frais comme des chairs d'enfants,
Doux comme les hautbois, verts comme les prairies,
—Et d'autres, corrompus, riches et triomphants,

Ayant l'expansion des choses infinies,
Comme l'ambre, le musc, le benjoin et l'encens,
Qui chantent les transports de l'esprit et des sens.

Correspondences

All Nature is a pillared temple where,
At times, live columns mutter words unclear;
Forests of symbols watch Man pass, and peer
With intimate glance and a familiar air.

Like distant, long-drawn calls that seem to be
Obscurely, deeply blended into one—
Vast as the dark of night and day's bright sun—
Sound, perfumes, hues echo in harmony.

Perfumes! Some fresh and cool, like babies' skin,
Mellow as oboes, green as meadows; some
Rich and exultant, decadent as sin,

Infinite in expanse—like benzoin gum,
Incense and amber, musk and benjamin—
Sing flesh's bliss, and soul's delight therein.

La Muse malade

Ma pauvre muse, hélas! qu'as-tu donc ce matin?
Tes yeux creux sont peuplés de visions nocturnes,
Et je vois tour à tour réfléchis sur ton teint
La folie et l'horreur, froides et taciturnes.

Le succube verdâtre et le rose lutin
T'ont-ils versé la peur et l'amour de leurs urnes?
Le cauchemar, d'un poing despotique et mutin,
T'a-t-il noyée au fond d'un fabuleux Minturnes?

Je voudrais qu'exhalant l'odeur de la santé
Ton sein de pensers forts fût toujours fréquenté,
Et que ton sang chrétien coulât à flots rythmiques

Comme les sons nombreux des syllabes antiques,
Où règnent tour à tour le père des chansons,
Phœbus, et le grand Pan, le seigneur des moissons.

The Sick Muse

Poor muse! What ails you in this day's new light?
Your hollow eyes teem with night-visions blear;
And in your sallow hue I see, now fright,
Now frenzy, mark your gaze: tight-lipped, austere.

Have glaucous succubus and pinkish sprite
Poured out on you their urns of love and fear?
Has spiteful-fisted nightmare drowned you quite,
Plunged deep in some Minturnean souvenir?

Rather might I prefer to see your breast
Filled with the breath of health, with vigorous thought;
To hear your Christian blood pound, as blood ought,

Like Ancients' dactyl, iamb, anapest,
Where Phoebus reigns, patron of song and rhyme,
And Pan, that great lord of the harvesttime.

Le Mauvais Moine

Les cloîtres anciens sur leurs grandes murailles
Etalaient en tableaux la sainte Vérité,
Dont l'effet, réchauffant les pieuses entrailles
Tempérait la froideur de leur austérité.

En ces temps où du Christ florissaient les semailles,
Plus d'un illustre moine, aujourd'hui peu cité,
Prenant pour atelier le champ des funérailles,
Glorifiait la Mort avec simplicité.

—Mon âme est un tombeau que, mauvais cénobite,
Depuis l'éternité je parcours et j'habite;
Rien n'embellit les murs de ce cloître odieux.

O moine fainéant! quand saurai-je donc faire
Du spectacle vivant de ma triste misère
Le travail de mes mains et l'amour de mes yeux?

The Wretched Monk

Our ancient cloisters' lofty walls displayed
The holy Truth, in sacred effigy,
That warmed the godly innards, and allayed
The coldness of their stark austerity.

Then many the famed, now unsung monk who made—
In days when thrived Christ's monkish progeny—
His workshop of the graveyard, and portrayed
Death's glory with an artless artistry.

—My soul, too, is a doleful hermit's tomb:
Home of my destiny and my foredoom,
With nothing to adorn my cloister bare.

O wretched monk! When will my own hands mold,
From the live spectacle of my despair,
Something my eyes might fancy to behold?

L'Ennemi

Ma jeunesse ne fut qu'un ténébreux orage,
Traversé çà et là par de brillants soleils;
Le tonnerre et la pluie ont fait un tel ravage,
Qu'il reste en mon jardin bien peu de fruits vermeils.

Voilà que j'ai touché l'automne des idées,
Et qu'il faut employer la pelle et les râteaux
Pour rassembler à neuf les terres inondées,
Où l'eau creuse des trous grands comme des tombeaux.

Et qui sait si les fleurs nouvelles que je rêve
Trouveront dans ce sol lavé comme une grève
Le mystique aliment qui ferait leur vigueur?

—O douleur! ô douleur! Le Temps mange la vie,
Et l'obscur Ennemi qui nous ronge le cœur
Du sang que nous perdons croît et se fortifie!

The Enemy

My youth was one long, dismal storm, shot through
Now and again with flashing suns; the rain
And thunder stripped my orchard bare: too few,
Today, the ruddy fruits that still remain.

And so I reach the autumn of my mind:
With rake and shovel must I now set out
To right the sodden landscape, where I find
Deep, gaping holes, like graves, dug roundabout.

But who knows if this soil, like sea-washed shore,
Will feed the new-dreamt flowers of my art
The mystic food their vigor hungers for?

—Ah woe! Ah woe! Time eats life to the core,
And the dark Enemy who gnaws our heart
Gluts on our blood and prospers all the more.

Le Guignon

Pour soulever un poids si lourd,
Sisyphe, il faudrait ton courage!
Bien qu'on ait du cœur à l'ouvrage,
L'Art est long et le Temps est court.

Loin des sépultures célèbres,
Vers un cimetière isolé,
Mon cœur, comme un tambour voilé,
Va battant des marches funèbres.

—Maint joyau dort enseveli
Dans les ténèbres et l'oubli,
Bien loin des pioches et des sondes;

Mainte fleur épanche à regret
Son parfum doux comme un secret
Dans les solitudes profondes.

The Jinx

Sisyphus, one must be as strong
And brave as you to lift this weight!
Though one be tireless, obdurate,
Yet Life is short and Art is long.

Far from the tombs of glorydom,
In some lone graveyard, set apart,
Beating the dead-man's-march, my heart
Pounds out its pace, like muffled drum.

—Many a gem lies buried deep
In darkness, overlooked, asleep,
Far from the pick and probe, alone.

Many a flower, alas, was meant
To spread the fragrance of its scent
In secret solitude, unknown.

La Vie antérieure

J'ai longtemps habité sous de vastes portiques
Que les soleils marins teignaient de mille feux,
Et que leurs grands piliers, droits et majestueux,
Rendaient pareils, le soir, aux grottes basaltiques.

Les houles, en roulant les images des cieux
Mêlaient d'une façon solennelle et mystique
Les tout-puissants accords de leur riche musique
Aux couleurs du couchant reflété par mes yeux.

C'est là que j'ai vécu dans les voluptés calmes,
Au milieu de l'azur, des vagues, des splendeurs
Et des esclaves nus, tout imprégnés d'odeurs,

Qui me rafraîchissaient le front avec des palmes,
Et dont l'unique soin était d'approfondir
Le secret douloureux qui me faisait languir.

The Former Life

Long did I live beneath vast colonnades—
Inflamed by sea sun's myriad rays, agleam—
Whose straight, tall, stately pillars made them seem
Like basalt grottoes in the twilight shades.

Sky patterns changed with every fall and rise;
Each surging swell that mingled solemnly
Its thunderous chords, in mystic harmony
With sunsets' hues reflected in my eyes.

There did I languish in a sensuous calm
Amid the azure-splendored skies and waves,
Pampered by naked, pungent-scented slaves,

Who fanned my languid brow with fronds of palm
To ease my secret anguish; their one care,
To plumb the hidden depths of my despair.

L'Homme et la mer

Homme libre, toujours tu chériras la mer!
La mer est ton miroir; tu contemples ton âme
Dans le déroulement infini de sa lame,
Et ton esprit n'est pas un gouffre moins amer.

Tu te plais à plonger au sein de ton image;
Tu l'embrasses des yeux et des bras, et ton cœur
Se distrait quelquefois de sa propre rumeur
Au bruit de cette plainte indomptable et sauvage.

Vous êtes tous les deux ténébreux et discrets:
Homme, nul n'a sondé le fond de tes abîmes,
O mer, nul ne connaît tes richesses intimes,
Tant vous êtes jaloux de garder vos secrets!

Et cependant voilà des siècles innombrables
Que vous vous combattez sans pitié ni remord,
Tellement vous aimez le carnage et la mort,
O lutteurs éternels, ô frères implacables!

Man and the Sea

Man, creature free, forever will you keep
The sea dear to your breast: your mirror. There,
In endless swell, you see your soul laid bare,
Gaze at your spirit's bitter, briny deep.

You plunge with joy into your own reflection,
Kiss it, embrace it with your arms, your eyes;
Your heart takes pleasure in its plaintive cries,
Wild, untamed clamor of its own dejection.

Both of you are discreet, dim, shadow-ridden:
Man, none has plumbed your soul's abyss; and, sea,
No one has pierced your wealth's dark mystery,
So jealous, you, to keep your treasures hidden!

Yet there you are, for centuries unending,
Pitilessly, remorselessly at war,
In love with carnage, death: forevermore
Eternal enemies, brothers unbending!

Frissonnant sous son deuil, la chaste et maigre Elvire

MI TRADÌ QUELL'ALMA INGRATA,
INFELICE, OH DIO, MI FA.
MA TRADITA E ABBANDONATA,
PROVO ANCOR PER LUI PIETÀ.

QUANDO SENTO IL MIO TORMENTO,
DI VENDETTA IL COR FAVELLA,
MA SE GUARDO IL SUO CIMENTO,
PALPITANDO IL COR MI VA.

Don Juan aux enfers

Quand Don Juan descendit vers l'onde souterraine
Et lorsqu'il eut donné son obole à Charon,
Un sombre mendiant, l'œil fier comme Antisthène,
D'un bras vengeur et fort saisit chaque aviron.

Montrant leurs seins pendants et leurs robes ouvertes
Des femmes se tordaient sous le noir firmament,
Et, comme un grand troupeau de victimes offertes,
Derrière lui traînaient un long mugissement.

Sganarelle en riant lui réclamait ses gages,
Tandis que Don Luis avec un doigt tremblant
Montrait à tous les morts errant sur les rivages
Le fils audacieux qui railla son front blanc.

Frissonnant sous son deuil, la chaste et maigre Elvire,
Près de l'époux perfide et qui fut son amant,
Semblait lui réclamer un suprême sourire
Où brillât la douceur de son premier serment.

Tout droit dans son armure, un grand homme de pierre
Se tenait à la barre et coupait le flot noir;
Mais le calme héros, courbé sur sa rapière,
Regardait le sillage et ne daignait rien voir.

Don Juan in Hell

When Don Juan, in his netherward descent,
Had paid Charon his toll by Stygian shore,
A doleful beggar—stout-armed, vengeance-bent,
Proud as Antisthenes—leered, seized each oar.

Women sprawled writhing, pendent bosoms bare,
Robes rent, beneath the black infernal sky;
Like sacrificial flock, they filled the air,
Trailing, in long lament, their woeful cry.

With laughing Sganarelle claiming his due,
Don Luis, among the dark banks' errant dead,
Trembling, marked out his son: base blackguard, who
Had heaped vile scorn upon his hoary head.

Shuddering in her weeds—chaste, gaunt—Elvire
Seemed to beg one more rapturous smile; somehow
To kindle once again the souvenir
Of faithless lover-husband's first sweet vow.

A great stone helmsman cleft the deep, arrayed—
Erect—in armor-plated panoply;
But calm, the hero, leaning on his blade,
Gazed at the wake through eyes that deigned not see.

Sale, inutile et laid comme une chose usée

Châtiment de l'orgueil

En ces temps merveilleux où la Théologie
Fleurit avec le plus de sève et d'énergie,
On raconte qu'un jour un docteur des plus grands,
—Après avoir forcé les cœurs indifférents;
Les avoir remués dans leurs profondeurs noires;
Après avoir franchi vers les célestes gloires
Des chemins singuliers à lui-même inconnus,
Où les purs Esprits seuls peut-être étaient venus,—
Comme un homme monté trop haut, pris de panique,
S'écria, transporté d'un orgueil satanique:
"Jésus, petit Jésus! je t'ai poussé bien haut!
Mais, si j'avais voulu t'attaquer au défaut
De l'armure, ta honte égalerait ta gloire,
Et tu ne serais plus qu'un fœtus dérisoire!"

Immédiatement sa raison s'en alla.
L'éclat de ce soleil d'un crêpe se voila;
Tout le chaos roula dans cette intelligence,
Temple autrefois vivant, plein d'ordre et d'opulence,
Sous les plafonds duquel tant de pompe avait lui.
Le silence et la nuit s'installèrent en lui,
Comme dans un caveau dont la clef est perdue.
Dès lors il fut semblable aux bêtes de la rue,
Et, quand il s'en allait sans rien voir, à travers
Les champs, sans distinguer les étés des hivers,
Sale, inutile et laid comme une chose usée,
Il faisait des enfants la joie et la risée.

Pride Punished

In days long past—that glorious, wondrous time,
Back when Theology was in its prime,
Filled with the sap of fresh and vigorous bloom—
They tell about a learned cleric whom
Great fame had marked; who, having stirred
Coldhearted unbelievers with The Word,
Deep in the darkness of their souls; and who,
Treading those heavenly pathways known unto
None but, perhaps, the purest Spirits, cried—
Suddenly moved by a Satanic pride,
Panicked, like one who dared to climb too high:
"Child Jesus! See how far I've raised you! Why,
Had I attacked your armor's flaw, great shame
Would surely have replaced your glorious name!
Merely a paltry foetus would you be!"

That said, he lost his reason, instantly.
His mind's resplendent sun stood veiled; his sense
Turned chaos. Once a living temple, whence
An ordered opulence had shone; now, nought
But night and silence in that mad, distraught,
Dungeon-like brain, keys nowhere to be found.
Thenceforth like stray beasts would he wander round
The streets and fields, most miserable of men,
Winter and summer, aimlessly. And when—
Vile, ugly, worthless wretch—he roamed about,
Children, laughing with glee, would point him out.

La Beauté

Je suis belle, ô mortels! comme un rêve de pierre,
Et mon sein, où chacun s'est meurtri tour à tour,
Est fait pour inspirer au poëte un amour
Eternel et muet ainsi que la matière.

Je trône dans l'azur comme un sphinx incompris;
J'unis un cœur de neige à la blancheur des cygnes;
Je hais le mouvement qui déplace les lignes,
Et jamais je ne pleure et jamais je ne ris.

Les poëtes, devant mes grandes attitudes,
Que j'ai l'air d'emprunter aux plus fiers monuments,
Consumeront leurs jours en d'austères études;

Car j'ai, pour fasciner ces dociles amants,
De purs miroirs qui font toutes choses plus belles:
Mes yeux, mes larges yeux aux clartés éternelles!

Beauty

I'm beautiful, O mortals, as might be
A sculpted dream; my bosom fine—whereof,
Bruised, all would suckle—fires the poet's love:
Silent as stone, fixed as eternity.

Like sphinx obscure, lording the azure, I
Join snow-cold heart to swans' sheer white; I scorn
Form's changing lines, of transient movement born,
And never do I laugh, and never cry.

Poets will spend their days, dour and intent,
Before my air aloof: haughty my pose,
Like pillar proud, toplofty monument.

For I possess pure mirror-eyes; yes, those
Wide eyes that charm these docile beaus, and render
All things more fair in their eternal splendor.

Tes appas façonnés aux bouches des Titans!

L'Idéal

Ce ne seront jamais ces beautés de vignettes,
Produits avariés, nés d'un siècle vaurien,
Ces pieds à brodequins, ces doigts à castagnettes,
Qui sauront satisfaire un cœur comme le mien.

Je laisse à Gavarni, poëte des chloroses,
Son troupeau gazouillant de beautés d'hôpital,
Car je ne puis trouver parmi ces pâles roses
Une fleur qui ressemble à mon rouge idéal.

Ce qu'il faut à ce cœur profond comme un abîme,
C'est vous, Lady Macbeth, âme puissante au crime,
Rêve d'Eschyle éclos au climat des autans;

Ou bien toi, grande Nuit, fille de Michel-Ange,
Qui tords paisiblement dans une pose étrange
Tes appas façonnés aux bouches des Titans!

The Ideal

A heart like mine will not be satisfied
With those vignette-style lovelies, weatherworn—
Fingers in castanets, feet tightly tied
In buskin-boots—of worthless century born.

I leave to Gavarni's anemic brush
His cooing flock of hospice belles—wan, weak:
I find among those roses' pallid blush
No bloom to match that red ideal I seek.

My chasm-heart needs Aeschylus to strew
Its unplumbed depths with ancient dream; like you,
Lady Macbeth, soul of foul crime impassioned;

Or you, Night—child of Michelangelo's
Begetting—who, in calm, eccentric pose,
Writhe with those charms for Titans' mouths once fashioned.

Dormir nonchalamment à l'ombre de ses seins

La Géante

Du temps que la Nature en sa verve puissante
Concevait chaque jour des enfants monstrueux,
J'eusse aimé vivre auprès d'une jeune géante,
Comme aux pieds d'une reine un chat voluptueux.

J'eusse aimé voir son corps fleurir avec son âme
Et grandir librement dans ses terribles jeux;
Deviner si son cœur couve une sombre flamme
Aux humides brouillards qui nagent dans ses yeux;

Parcourir à loisir ses magnifiques formes;
Ramper sur le versant de ses genoux énormes,
Et parfois en été, quand les soleils malsains,

Lasse, la font s'étendre à travers la campagne,
Dormir nonchalamment à l'ombre de ses seins,
Comme un hameau paisible au pied d'une montagne.

The Giantess

Back when a bustling Nature, limitless,
Each day spawned a new offspring oddity,
Ah, to have dwelt by some young giantess,
Like cat at queen's feet, nestling lustfully.

Ah, to have watched her soul and body bloom,
Amid her awesome games, in wanton wise;
Sensed her heart's muted flames, nursed in the gloom,
Smouldering in her moist, mist-clouded eyes;

To browse her grandiose shapes; to take my ease
Crawling high on her huge-sloped thighs and knees;
Or, when the summer's blistering suns had made

Her sprawl across the countryside, hard put,
Ah, but to slumber in her bosom's shade:
A hamlet calm, tucked at the mountain's foot.

Hymne à la beauté

Viens-tu du ciel profond ou sors-tu de l'abîme,
O Beauté? ton regard, infernal et divin,
Verse confusément le bienfait et le crime,
Et l'on peut pour cela te comparer au vin.

Tu contiens dans ton œil le couchant et l'aurore;
Tu répands des parfums comme un soir orageux;
Tes baisers sont un philtre et ta bouche une amphore
Qui font le héros lâche et l'enfant courageux.

Sors-tu du gouffre noir ou descends-tu des astres?
Le Destin charmé suit tes jupons comme un chien;
Tu sèmes au hasard la joie et les désastres,
Et tu gouvernes tout et ne réponds de rien.

Tu marches sur les morts, Beauté, dont tu te moques;
De tes bijoux l'Horreur n'est pas le moins charmant,
Et le Meurtre, parmi tes plus chères breloques,
Sur ton ventre orgueilleux danse amoureusement.

L'éphémère ébloui vole vers toi, chandelle,
Crépite, flambe et dit: Bénissons ce flambeau!
L'amoureux pantelant incliné sur sa belle
A l'air d'un moribond caressant son tombeau.

Que tu viennes du ciel ou de l'enfer, qu'importe,
O Beauté! monstre énorme, effrayant, ingénu!
Si ton œil, ton souris, ton pied, m'ouvrent la porte
D'un Infini que j'aime et n'ai jamais connu?

De Satan ou de Dieu, qu'importe? Ange ou Sirène,
Qu'importe, si tu rends,—fée aux yeux de velours,
Rythme, parfums, lueur, ô mon unique reine!—
L'univers moins hideux et les instants moins lourds?

Hymn to Beauty

O Beauty! Do you come from dark abyss
Or from empyrean heights? Your glance—divine,
Infernal—pours a blend of heaven's bliss
And hell's debauch; indeed, not unlike wine.

Sunset and dawn shine in your gaze; you waft
Perfumes, like evening winds, gusting about;
Your mouth: a vase; your kiss: a witching draught
That turns the hero meek, the weak lad stout.

Whence do you come? Black pit or star-deep sky?
Fate dogs your skirts, possessed; you govern him
And everything, with none to question why,
Dealing out grief and joy quite at your whim.

You tread upon the dead with carefree stride:
Horror is not your least seductive frill;
Lovingly, on your belly puffed with pride,
Murder—rich bauble—trips a light quadrille.

Dazzled, the mayfly cries: "O firebrand blest!"
And, crackling in your candle, seeks its doom.
The lover, panting on his mistress' breast,
Is like the man near death, who hugs his tomb.

Monster naive and fearsome, whence of late
You come, O Beauty, matters not a whit,
If your eyes, smile, feet open wide the gate,
At last, unto my longed-for Infinite.

Angel or Siren? God- or Satan-sent?
What difference, if—down-eyed divinity,
My queen—your scents, sights, rhythms represent
Solace from ugliness and life's ennui?

Parfum exotique

Quand, les deux yeux fermés, en un soir chaud d'automne,
Je respire l'odeur de ton sein chaleureux,
Je vois se dérouler des rivages heureux,
Qu'éblouissent les feux d'un soleil monotone:

Une île paresseuse où la nature donne
Des arbres singuliers et des fruits savoureux;
Des hommes dont le corps est mince et vigoureux,
Et des femmes dont l'œil par sa franchise étonne.

Guidé par ton odeur vers de charmants climats,
Je vois un port rempli de voiles et de mâts
Encor tout fatigués par la vague marine,

Pendant que le parfum des verts tamariniers,
Qui circule dans l'air et m'enfle la narine,
Se mêle dans mon âme au chant des mariniers.

Exotic Perfume

When, on our late, hot autumn afternoons,
Eyes closed, I breathe your breast's warm, heady scent,
I see a sun, fixed in the firmament,
Shining on dazzling shores: strand, rolling dunes;

One of those lazy, nature-gifted isles,
With luscious fruits, trees strange of leaf and limb,
Men vigorous of body, lithe and slim,
Women with artless glance that awes, beguiles.

Lured by your scent, led on to charming clime,
I come upon a port, all mast and sail,
Battered and buffeted by tide and time;

And all the while green tamarinds exhale
Perfumes that fill my nostrils and my soul,
Blending with sounds of sailors' barcarole.

La Chevelure

O toison, moutonnant jusque sur l'encolure!
O boucles! O parfum chargé de nonchaloir!
Extase! Pour peupler ce soir l'alcôve obscure
Des souvenirs dormant dans cette chevelure,
Je la veux agiter dans l'air comme un mouchoir!

La langoureuse Asie et la brûlante Afrique,
Tout un monde lointain, absent, presque défunt,
Vit dans tes profondeurs, forêt aromatique!
Comme d'autres esprits voguent sur la musique,
Le mien, ô mon amour! nage sur ton parfum.

J'irai là-bas où l'arbre et l'homme, pleins de sève,
Se pâment longuement sous l'ardeur des climats;
Fortes tresses, soyez la houle qui m'enlève!
Tu contiens, mer d'ébène, un éblouissant rêve
De voiles, de rameurs, de flammes et de mâts:

Un port retentissant où mon âme peut boire
A grands flots le parfum, le son et la couleur;
Où les vaisseaux, glissant dans l'or et dans la moire,
Ouvrent leurs vastes bras pour embrasser la gloire
D'un ciel pur où frémit l'éternelle chaleur.

Je plongerai ma tête amoureuse d'ivresse
Dans ce noir océan où l'autre est enfermé;
Et mon esprit subtil que le roulis caresse
Saura vous retrouver, ô féconde paresse,
Infinis bercements du loisir embaumé!

Cheveux bleus, pavillon de ténèbres tendues,
Vous me rendez l'azur du ciel immense et rond;
Sur les bords duvetés de vos mèches tordues

Tresses

O fleece! Curls rippling round the shoulders! Hair
Thick with the scent of languorous perfume!
What bliss! To shake it, kerchief-like—here, there;
Wake sleeping memories, waft them through the air,
Filling, this night, our alcove's darkling gloom.

Continents, worlds, distant and dying, lie
Deep in your forest, lush and redolent:
Orient's torpor, Africa's parched sky!
Some souls drift free on music, Love; but I
Float on the musky fragrance of your scent.

There will I go, where sap-rich man and tree
Laze, swooning, in the heat, days upon days.
Powerful tresses! Swell—O ebony sea!—
And sweep me off, there, to that fantasy
Within you: sails, masts, oarsmen, bright ablaze;

A clamorous port to sate me, thirsty-souled,
Where I may gorge on smell, and sound, and hue;
Where boats, gliding on silk-glossed waves of gold,
Lift arms to sky's pure glory, to enfold
Its heat eternal, shimmering in the blue.

Then will I plunge my head, in drunken quest,
Into that dark sea where the other lies;
My lucent soul will loll, wave-cradled, crest
To crest—O fertile languor!—balm-caressed,
Rocked, ever anon, midst silent lullabies.

O sea-blue locks! O pennon shadow-spread!
About your downy ringlets, intertwined,
Sprawls heaven's vast-vaulted azure, overhead;

Je m'enivre ardemment des senteurs confondues
De l'huile de coco, du musc et du goudron.

Longtemps! toujours! ma main dans ta crinière lourde
Sèmera le rubis, la perle et le saphir,
Afin qu'à mon désir tu ne sois jamais sourde!
N'es-tu pas l'oasis où je rêve, et la gourde
Où je hume à longs traits le vin du souvenir?

And I glut, drunk with pleasure, surfeited
On scents of palm oil, pitch, and musk combined.

Forever! Let me strew that fleece, in turn—
That mane!—with ruby, pearl, and sapphire fine!
Then never will you scoff my passion, spurn
My love! You, dream-oasis? You, the urn
Whence I quaff deep the draughts of memory's wine?

Je t'adore à l'égal de la voûte nocturne,
O vase de tristesse, ô grande taciturne,
Et t'aime d'autant plus, belle, que tu me fuis,
Et que tu me parais, ornement de mes nuits,
Plus ironiquement accumuler les lieues
Qui séparent mes bras des immensités bleues.

Je m'avance à l'attaque, et je grimpe aux assauts,
Comme après un cadavre un chœur de vermisseaux.
Et je chéris, ô bête implacable et cruelle!
Jusqu'à cette froideur par où tu m'es plus belle!

"I worship you like heaven's dark vault, O urn... "

I worship you like heaven's dark vault, O urn
Of wistfulness, grand beauty taciturn,
And love you all the more—jewel of my night—
The more you scorn, the more you take your flight,
League upon league, leaving me, as you do,
To yearn in vain for realms of endless blue.

I rise to your attack, in humble wise,
Crawling like host of worms that gormandize
Some rotting corpse, and prize that cold, harsh air—
O creature cruel!—that makes you yet more fair.

53

Tu mettrais l'univers entier dans ta ruelle

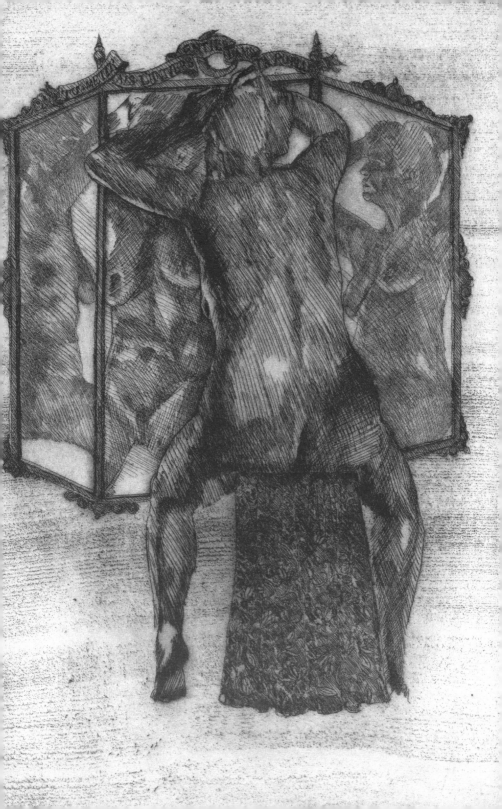

Tu mettrais l'univers entier dans ta ruelle,
Femme impure! L'ennui rend ton âme cruelle.
Pour exercer tes dents à ce jeu singulier,
Il te faut chaque jour un cœur au râtelier.
Tes yeux, illuminés ainsi que des boutiques
Et des ifs flamboyants dans les fêtes publiques,
Usent insolemment d'un pouvoir emprunté,
Sans connaître jamais la loi de leur beauté.

Machine aveugle et sourde, en cruauté féconde!
Salutaire instrument, buveur du sang du monde,
Comment n'as-tu pas honte et comment n'as-tu pas
Devant tous les miroirs vu pâlir tes appas?
La grandeur de ce mal où tu te crois savante
Ne t'a donc jamais fait reculer d'épouvante,
Quand la nature, grande en ses desseins cachés,
De toi se sert, ô femme, ô reine des péchés,
—De toi, vil animal,—pour pétrir un génie?

O fangeuse grandeur! sublime ignominie!

56

"Boredom it is that breeds your vicious soul... "

Boredom it is that breeds your vicious soul,
Vile woman! You who well would bed the whole
Wide world. For, in your quaint and curious play,
Your jaws must find a heart to crush each day.
And, if your teeth would ply their wicked game,
Your eyes, like festive-candled yews, aflame
With light, or like shopwindows bright ablaze,
Borrow a power to fire their haughty gaze,
With never a notion of their beauty's might.

Blind, deaf machine, rich in cruel appetite,
Device to suck Man's blood! For shame! How do
Your looking-glasses not reveal to you
Your fading charms? Have you not once recoiled
To see yourself by evil thus despoiled—
Evil in which you deem yourself expert—
When blithely nature chooses to pervert
Your woman's flesh—foul beast, O queen of sin;
To shape and mold a genie-sprite therein,
And use you to perform her deviltry?

O squalid grandeur! lofty infamy!

Sed non satiata

Bizarre déité, brune comme les nuits,
Au parfum mélangé de musc et de havane,
Œuvre de quelque obi, le Faust de la savane,
Sorcière au flanc d'ébène, enfant des noirs minuits,

Je préfère au constance, à l'opium, au nuits,
L'élixir de ta bouche où l'amour se pavane;
Quand vers toi mes désirs partent en caravane,
Tes yeux sont la citerne où boivent mes ennuis.

Par ces deux grands yeux noirs, soupiraux de ton âme,
O démon sans pitié! verse-moi moins de flamme;
Je ne suis pas le Styx pour t'embrasser neuf fois,

Hélas! et je ne puis, Mégère libertine,
Pour briser ton courage et te mettre aux abois,
Dans l'enfer de ton lit devenir Proserpine!

Sed non satiata

Strange goddess, tawny as the dusk, you come
Swathed in lush smoke, in musk; and I surmise
Some grassland Faust sired you in wizard wise,
Ebon-flanked witch, spawned of night's shadowdom.

More than old, heady wines, or opium,
I crave your lips' elixir: proud love's prize;
And when my lusts trek after you, your eyes
Are wells where drinks my desert's tedium.

Let those dark eyes, I pray, rain on me less
Of your soul's flame, cruel demon-sorceress;
No Styx am I, able to circle you

Nine times around; nor can I—wanton shrew,
Megaera mine!—bring you to heel, and be,
In your bed's hell, a new Persephone!

Avec ses vêtements ondoyants et nacrés,
Même quand elle marche on croirait qu'elle danse,
Comme ces longs serpents que les jongleurs sacrés
Au bout de leurs bâtons agitent en cadence.

Comme le sable morne et l'azur des déserts,
Insensibles tous deux à l'humaine souffrance,
Comme les longs réseaux de la houle des mers,
Elle se développe avec indifférence.

Ses yeux polis sont faits de minéraux charmants,
Et dans cette nature étrange et symbolique
Où l'ange inviolé se mêle au sphinx antique,

Où tout n'est qu'or, acier, lumière et diamants,
Resplendit à jamais, comme un astre inutile,
La froide majesté de la femme stérile.

"Dressed in her opalescent, shimmering clothes... "

Dressed in her opalescent, shimmering clothes,
Even her walk is like a dance, as she
Moves with her smoothly measured gait, like those
Stick-snakes that holy jugglers dangle free.

Like desert sands and skies, untouched by woes
Of mankind and its human misery;
Like sea of endless-rolling waves, she goes
Wending her way, coldly, indifferently.

Her brilliant eyes shine their bewitching ore;
And in that wondrous strange symbolic creature,
Blending the angel pure and sphinx of yore—

All steel, gold, diamonds, light, her every feature—
Gleams like a star, barren but glimmering still,
The sterile woman's vain, majestic chill.

De profundis clamavi

J'implore ta pitié, Toi, l'unique que j'aime,
Du fond du gouffre obscur où mon cœur est tombé.
C'est un univers morne à l'horizon plombé,
Où nagent dans la nuit l'horreur et le blasphème;

Un soleil sans chaleur plane au-dessus six mois,
Et les six autres mois la nuit couvre la terre;
C'est un pays plus nu que la terre polaire;
—Ni bêtes, ni ruisseaux, ni verdure, ni bois!

Or il n'est pas d'horreur au monde qui surpasse
La froide cruauté de ce soleil de glace
Et cette immense nuit semblable au vieux Chaos;

Je jalouse le sort des plus vils animaux
Qui peuvent se plonger dans un sommeil stupide,
Tant l'écheveau du temps lentement se dévide!

De profundis clamavi

From my abysmal depths, I cry: "You, whom
Alone I love, have pity!" Here my heart
Swims in a lead-skied universe, apart,
Awash in horror, blasphemy, and doom.

A heatless sun hangs over half the year.
The other half, night cloaks the landscape round,
More naked than a barren arctic ground:
No living thing, plant, river, forest here!

There is no horror on this earth more cold,
More heartless than that lifeless, ice-bound sun,
And that deep night, like Chaos-days of old.

How slowly does time's skein unwind! Ah me,
Would I were like those beasts that, mindlessly,
Sink into slumber, sleep till time is done!

Toi qui, comme un coup de couteau,

Dans mon cœur plaintif es entrée

Le Vampire

Toi qui, comme un coup de couteau,
Dans mon cœur plaintif es entrée;
Toi qui, forte comme un troupeau
De démons, vins, folle et parée,

De mon esprit humilié
Faire ton lit et ton domaine;
—Infâme à qui je suis lié
Comme le forçat à la chaîne,

Comme au jeu le joueur têtu,
Comme à la bouteille l'ivrogne,
Comme aux vermines la charogne,
—Maudite, maudite sois-tu!

J'ai prié le glaive rapide
De conquérir ma liberté,
Et j'ai dit au poison perfide
De secourir ma lâcheté.

Hélas! le poison et le glaive
M'ont pris en dédain et m'ont dit:
"Tu n'es pas digne qu'on t'enlève
A ton esclavage maudit,

Imbécile!—de son empire
Si nos efforts te délivraient,
Tes baisers ressusciteraient
Le cadavre de ton vampire!"

The Vampire

You who came plunging like a knife
Into my heart, sore with chagrin;
Who, daft and frilled, attacked my life
Like demon horde let loose therein,

To turn my humbled soul and mind
Into your bed and your domain:
—Monster, who shackle me and bind
Me fast, like convict to his chain,

Like drunkard to his gin and wine,
Like hardened gambler to his dice,
Like carrion swill to worms and lice,
—Damn you! Be damned, vile mistress mine!

I begged the sword's swift blade to ease
My pain, and end my soul's duress;
I bade perfidious poison, please
Come save me from this wretchedness.

But blade and poison, in reply,
Turned to me with disdainful sneer
And mouthed their scornful answer: "Why?
You're not worth saving, fool!" they jeer.

"Imbecile! If, from her control,
Our efforts were to succor you,
Your kisses would raise up anew
Your vampire's corpse, live, hale and whole."

"Une nuit que j'étais près d'une affreuse Juive... "

Une nuit que j'étais près d'une affreuse Juive,
Comme au long d'un cadavre un cadavre étendu,
Je me pris à songer près de ce corps vendu
A la triste beauté dont mon désir se prive.

Je me représentai sa majesté native,
Son regard de vigueur et de grâces armé,
Ses cheveux qui lui font un casque parfumé,
Et dont le souvenir pour l'amour me ravive.

Car j'eusse avec ferveur baisé ton noble corps,
Et depuis tes pieds frais jusqu'à tes noires tresses
Déroulé le trésor des profondes caresses,

Si, quelque soir, d'un pleur obtenu sans effort
Tu pouvais seulement, ô reine des cruelles!
Obscurcir la splendeur de tes froides prunelles.

"One night, with a vile Jewess by my side... "

One night, with a vile Jewess by my side,
Pressed to that hired flesh, sharing my bed,
Lying like corpse to corpse, dreams filled my head,
Of the chill beauty to my lust denied.

My mind's eye saw her air of stately pride,
Her look armed with an energetic grace,
Her hair, a scented cloche framing her face,
Waking my heart to love, soul-satisfied.

For I would kiss your noble form; caress,
Lavish on you my passion's boon profound,
From tender feet to head, black tresses-crowned,

If, one night, you might shed—O merciless,
Cruel vixen queen!—one artless tear, perchance,
To dim the frigid radiance of your glance.

Viens, mon beau chat, sur mon cœur amoureux

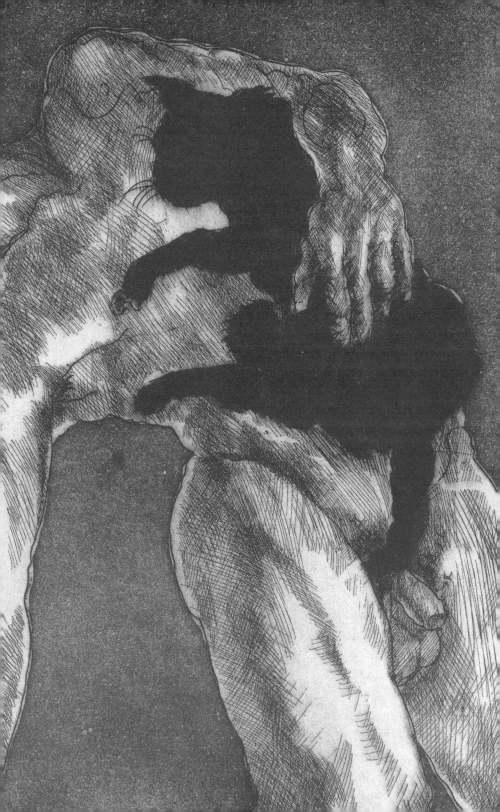

Le Chat

Viens, mon beau chat, sur mon cœur amoureux;
    Retiens les griffes de ta patte,
Et laisse-moi plonger dans tes beaux yeux,
    Mêlés de métal et d'agate.

Lorsque mes doigts caressent à loisir
    Ta tête et ton dos élastique,
Et que ma main s'enivre du plaisir
    De palper ton corps électrique,

Je vois ma femme en esprit. Son regard,
    Comme le tien, aimable bête,
Profond et froid, coupe et fend comme un dard,

    Et, des pieds jusques à la tête,
Un air subtil, un dangereux parfum,
    Nagent autour de son corps brun.

The Cat

Come, cat of mine, perch on my loving breast;
 Come, beauty, lie in gentle guise:
Pull in your claws, and let me plunge, possessed,
 Into your agate-metal eyes.

When, to my hands' content, I pat your head,
 Fondle your neck, your back; and when
I paw your supple loins, bliss-surfeited,
 Stroke your electric fur; ah, then

My mistress springs to mind. I see her there,
 Darting at me her cold, deep stare,
As you do, my delightful pet, just so;

 And a stark fragrance—redolent,
Subtle and dangerous—from head to toe,
 Bathes her dark body in its scent.

Le Possédé

Le soleil s'est couvert d'un crêpe. Comme lui,
O Lune de ma vie! emmitoufle-toi d'ombre;
Dors ou fume à ton gré; sois muette, sois sombre,
Et plonge tout entière au gouffre de l'Ennui;

Je t'aime ainsi! Pourtant, si tu veux aujourd'hui,
Comme un astre éclipsé qui sort de la pénombre,
Te pavaner aux lieux que la Folie encombre,
C'est bien! Charmant poignard, jaillis de ton étui!

Allume ta prunelle à la flamme des lustres!
Allume le désir dans les regards des rustres!
Tout de toi m'est plaisir, morbide ou pétulant;

Sois ce que tu voudras, nuit noire, rouge aurore;
Il n'est pas une fibre en tout mon corps tremblant
Qui ne crie: *O mon cher Belzébuth, je t'adore!*

The Possessed

The sun is swathed in mourning, faintly lit.
Moon, my beloved, shroud yourself like him;
Smoke, sleep, as you prefer; be still, be dim,
And plunge into Ennui's deep-yawning pit.

So would I have you! But, if you see fit,
Like star eclipsed, to quit the shadows grim
And strut where Folly bubbles to the brim,
Fine! Strip your dagger's sheath: no need for it!

Let festive candle-flames brighten your eyes!
Let lust for you light bumpkins' gaze! For me,
Sullen or sprightly, you please equally.

Be what you will: night's black or dawn's red skies;
No fiber is there in my being but cries,
Trembling: "O Beelzebub, I worship thee!"

Le Démon, dans ma chambre haute,

Ce matin est venu me voir

Tout entière

Le Démon, dans ma chambre haute,
Ce matin est venu me voir,
Et, tâchant à me prendre en faute,
Me dit: "Je voudrais bien savoir,

Parmi toutes les belles choses
Dont est fait son enchantement,
Parmi les objets noirs ou roses
Qui composent son corps charmant,

Quel est le plus doux."—O mon âme!
Tu répondis à l'Abhorré:
"Puisqu'en Elle tout est dictame,
Rien ne peut être préféré.

Lorsque tout me ravit, j'ignore
Si quelque chose me séduit.
Elle éblouit comme l'Aurore
Et console comme la Nuit;

Et l'harmonie est trop exquise,
Qui gouverne tout son beau corps,
Pour que l'impuissante analyse
En note les nombreux accords.

O métamorphose mystique
De tous mes sens fondus en un!
Son haleine fait la musique,
Comme sa voix fait le parfum!"

All of Her

This morning, as I lay abed,
The Devil came to pay a call;
And, with a mind to trick me, said:
"Please tell me, if you can, of all

The many things that make her so
Enticing, charming in your sight;
Of all those darks and pinks that go
To form her body's sheer delight,

Which is the fairest?" "Glory be!"
My soul, you told the Fiend. "The best?
Her whole being pleasures, comforts me;
No part is fairer than the rest.

How should I say which lovely one
Enchants me most, deserves the palm?
She dazzles like the dawning sun,
Solaces like the evening's calm.

Were I to study, part by part,
Her beauty's music exquisite,
Too rich its notes, its chords: no art
Could analyze the whole of it!

O mystic blend of senses mine,
Fused in one perfect harmony!
Her voice, a fragrant perfume fine;
Her breath, the sweetest melody!"

Que diras-tu ce soir, pauvre âme solitaire,
Que diras-tu, mon cœur, cœur autrefois flétri,
A la très-belle, à la très-bonne, à la très-chère,
Dont le regard divin t'a soudain refleuri?

—Nous mettrons notre orgueil à chanter ses louanges:
Rien ne vaut la douceur de son autorité;
Sa chair spirituelle a le parfum des Anges,
Et son œil nous revêt d'un habit de clarté.

Que ce soit dans la nuit et dans la solitude.
Que ce soit dans la rue et dans la multitude,
Son fantôme dans l'air danse comme un flambeau.

Parfois il parle et dit: "Je suis belle, et j'ordonne
Que pour l'amour de moi vous n'aimiez que le Beau;
Je suis l'Ange gardien, la Muse et la Madone!"

"What will you say, once withered heart of mine... "

What will you say, once withered heart of mine;
What will you say tonight, poor soul forlorn,
To her—all sweetness, light—whose glance divine
Suddenly bloomed you back to life, reborn?

—Proudly, together, we will glorify
Her peerless power sublime, and sing her praise:
Her flesh is like the Angels', and we lie
Clothed in the pure transparence of her gaze.

Be it in darkling solitude of night,
Be it on multitudinous city street,
Her specter flames, a-dance on flickering feet,

Ordering me, at times: "My acolyte!
Love Beauty for the love and likes of me:
Your Virgin, Muse, and guardian Deity."

Le Flambeau vivant

Ils marchent devant moi, ces Yeux pleins de lumières,
Qu'un Ange très savant a sans doute aimantés;
Ils marchent, ces divins frères qui sont mes frères,
Secouant dans mes yeux leurs feux diamantés.

Me sauvant de tout piége et de tout péché grave,
Ils conduisent mes pas dans la route du Beau;
Ils sont mes serviteurs et je suis leur esclave;
Tout mon être obéit à ce vivant flambeau.

Charmants Yeux, vous brillez de la clarté mystique
Qu'ont les cierges brûlant en plein jour; le soleil
Rougit, mais n'éteint pas leur flamme fantastique;

Ils célèbrent la Mort, vous chantez le Réveil;
Vous marchez en chantant le réveil de mon âme,
Astres dont nul soleil ne peut flétrir la flamme!

The Living Torch

They march before me, those Eyes filled with light,
Made magnets, likely, by some angel wise;
They march, those heavenly twins, my brethren bright,
Strewing their diamond-fires into my eyes.

Keeping me safe from snares iniquitous,
They lead me in the path of Beauty; they
Are both my servants and my masters; thus
Does my whole being this living torch obey.

Bewitching eyes, you glow with mystic blaze,
Like tapers burning in the sun, whose rays
Never can dim their flame fantastic, pure;

But they chant Death, you sing Awakening:
Yes, as you march, my waking soul you sing,
O stars whose flame no sunlight can obscure!

Réversibilité

Ange plein de gaieté, connaissez-vous l'angoisse,
La honte, les remords, les sanglots, les ennuis,
Et les vagues terreurs de ces affreuses nuits
Qui compriment le cœur comme un papier qu'on froisse?
Ange plein de gaieté, connaissez-vous l'angoisse?

Ange plein de bonté, connaissez-vous la haine,
Les poings crispés dans l'ombre et les larmes de fiel,
Quand la Vengeance bat son infernal rappel,
Et de nos facultés se fait le capitaine?
Ange plein de bonté, connaissez-vous la haine?

Ange plein de santé, connaissez-vous les Fièvres,
Qui, le long des grands murs de l'hospice blafard,
Comme des exilés, s'en vont d'un pied traînard,
Cherchant le soleil rare et remuant les lèvres?
Ange plein de santé, connaissez-vous les Fièvres?

Ange plein de beauté, connaissez-vous les rides,
Et la peur de vieillir, et ce hideux tourment
De lire la secrète horreur du dévouement
Dans des yeux où longtemps burent nos yeux avides?
Ange plein de beauté, connaissez-vous les rides?

Ange plein de bonheur, de joie et de lumières,
David mourant aurait demandé la santé
Aux émanations de ton corps enchanté;
Mais de toi je n'implore, ange, que tes prières,
Ange plein de bonheur, de joie et de lumières!

Reversibility

Angel of gladness, do you know that smart,
Those conscience pangs, the woes, the sobs, the shame,
All the night's hideous fears without a name,
That squeeze, and press, and crumple up our heart?
Angel of gladness, do you know that smart?

Angel of goodness, do you know that hate—
Fist clenched in shadows grim, eyes weeping gall—
When Vengeance sounds his hell-bent battle call,
Our senses' captain, vile old reprobate?
Angel of goodness, do you know that hate?

Angel of vigor, do you know those Ills
That limp along dank hospice walls—bleak, stark—
Like exiles muttering silence in the dark,
Seeking the sun to ease their fevers, chills?
Angel of vigor, do you know those Ills?

Angel of beauty, do you know those signs
Of dreaded age, secrets no eye can keep
Concealed; age that torments with wrinkles, lines;
Eyes where our eyes once drank of passion deep?
Angel of beauty, do you know those signs?

Angel of wisdom, joy, prosperity,
They say that David, close to death, implored
Your holy radiance for his health restored;
I beg you only that you pray for me,
Angel of wisdom, joy, prosperity.

L'Aube spirituelle

Quand chez les débauchés l'aube blanche et vermeille
Entre en société de l'Idéal rongeur,
Par l'opération d'un mystère vengeur
Dans la brute assoupie un ange se réveille.

Des Cieux Spirituels l'inaccessible azur,
Pour l'homme terrassé qui rêve encore et souffre,
S'ouvre et s'enfonce avec l'attirance du gouffre.
Ainsi, chère Déesse, Etre lucide et pur,

Sur les débris fumeux des stupides orgies
Ton souvenir plus clair, plus rose, plus charmant,
A mes yeux agrandis voltige incessamment.

Le soleil a noirci la flamme des bougies;
Ainsi, toujours vainqueur, ton fantôme est pareil,
Ame resplendissante, à l'immortel soleil!

Dawn of the Spirit

When, by the workings of some dark, obscure
Accord with pink-white dawn, the pure Ideal
Gnaws at the libertine with vengeful zeal,
An angel wakens in the slumberous boor.

Distant, aloof, the azure, Heaven-graced,
Drawn toward the chasm, opens wide, redeems
Man the abject, still dreaming tortured dreams.
So too, dear Goddess, Creature bright and chaste,

The thought of you—rose-hued, sublime—shines clear,
Hovers before my wide-eyed gaze, above
The steaming waste of mindless orgy-love.

The sun mutes candles black, splendorous sphere!
And you, triumphant spirit-form, are one,
O radiant light, with the immortal sun!

Harmonie du soir

Voici venir les temps où vibrant sur sa tige
Chaque fleur s'évapore ainsi qu'un encensoir;
Les sons et les parfums tournent dans l'air du soir;
Valse mélancolique et langoureux vertige!

Chaque fleur s'évapore ainsi qu'un encensoir;
Le violon frémit comme un cœur qu'on afflige;
Valse mélancolique et langoureux vertige!
Le ciel est triste et beau comme un grand reposoir.

Le violon frémit comme un cœur qu'on afflige,
Un cœur tendre, qui hait le néant vaste et noir!
Le ciel est triste et beau comme un grand reposoir;
Le soleil s'est noyé dans son sang qui se fige.

Un cœur tendre, qui hait le néant vaste et noir,
Du passé lumineux recueille tout vestige!
Le soleil s'est noyé dans son sang qui se fige...
Ton souvenir en moi luit comme un ostensoir!

Evening Harmony

Now come the hours when, swaying stem-bent, lo!
Like censers, flowers spread fragrance everywhere;
Perfumes and sounds dance on the evening air;
Grave, wistful waltz, languorous vertigo.

Like censers, flowers spread fragrance everywhere;
A violin sobs its heartfelt tremolo;
Grave, wistful waltz, languorous vertigo!
Shrine-like, the heavens shine beauty's sad despair.

A violin sobs its heartfelt tremolo:
Kind heart that loathes the void—vast, black, and bare!
Shrine-like, the heavens shine beauty's sad despair;
The sun drowns in its clotting blood-red glow.

Kind heart that loathes the void—vast, black, and bare—
Gleans the last gleaming scraps of long ago!
The sun drowns in its clotting blood-red glow...
Like monstrance bright you light my thought, my prayer!

Le Poison

Le vin sait revêtir le plus sordide bouge
      D'un luxe miraculeux,
Et fait surgir plus d'un portique fabuleux
      Dans l'or de sa vapeur rouge,
Comme un soleil couchant dans un ciel nébuleux.

L'opium agrandit ce qui n'a pas de bornes,
      Allonge l'illimité
Approfondit le temps, creuse la volupté,
      Et de plaisirs noirs et mornes
Remplit l'âme au delà de sa capacité.

Tout cela ne vaut pas le poison qui découle
      De tes yeux, de tes yeux verts,
Lacs où mon âme tremble et se voit à l'envers...
      Mes songes viennent en foule
Pour se désaltérer à ces gouffres amers.

Tout cela ne vaut pas le terrible prodige
      De ta salive qui mord,
Qui plonge dans l'oubli mon âme sans remord,
      Et, charriant le vertige,
La roule défaillante aux rives de la mort!

Poison

Wine can adorn the brothel vile in clothes
    Of wondrous opulence; and it
Can conjure up, like cloud-decked heavens, lit
    By setting sun, dream-porticoes
Of vaporous reds and golds, hues exquisite.

Opium magnifies the limitless
    Beyond the infinite; it renders
Time fathomless, plumbs to our sensuousness,
    And, in our glutted soul, engenders
Morbid delights in black and vast excess.

Neither compares to that fell poison, springing
    Full from your eyes; green eyes accursed:
Lakes where I see my soul, in pose reversed,
    Trembling, and where my dreams come winging
Many a time and oft to slake their thirst.

Neither compares to your moist tongue, a-steep
    In spittle—awesome, venomous—
That plunges my remorseless spirit deep
    Into forgetfulness, and thus
Whisks it toward death's dark shores in dizzying sweep.

Ciel brouillé

On dirait ton regard d'une vapeur couvert;
Ton œil mystérieux (est-il bleu, gris ou vert?)
Alternativement tendre, rêveur, cruel,
Réfléchit l'indolence et la pâleur du ciel.

Tu rappelles ces jours blancs, tièdes et voilés,
Qui font se fondre en pleurs les cœurs ensorcelés,
Quand, agités d'un mal inconnu qui les tord,
Les nerfs trop éveillés raillent l'esprit qui dort.

Tu ressembles parfois à ces beaux horizons
Qu'allument les soleils des brumeuses saisons...
Comme tu resplendis, paysage mouillé
Qu'enflamment les rayons tombant d'un ciel brouillé!

O femme dangereuse, ô séduisants climats!
Adorerai-je aussi ta neige et vos frimas,
Et saurai-je tirer de l'implacable hiver
Des plaisirs plus aigus que la glace et le fer?

Heavens' Haze

That glance of yours seems veiled in mist; your eye
Mirrors the indolent and pallid sky—
Mystery-shrouded eye (blue, gray, or green?)—
Now cruel, now tender, musing, and serene.

You call to mind those days, cloud-white and mild,
That melt to tears hearts witchery-beguiled,
When, wide awake and racked by some vague ill,
Nerves taunt and twit the spirit, slumbering, still.

You look, at times, like those horizons fair
Whose fogbound suns shine through the murky air...
Landscape bedewed, you gleam beneath their rays
Of splendorous flame, rained from the heavens' haze!

Perilous woman! Climes that lure, entice!
Shall I love, too, your snow? Their hoary ice?
And draw from winter's chill—harsh, unallayed—
Pleasures more biting than the frost and blade?

Tu fais l'effet d'un beau vaisseau qui prend le large,

Chargé de toile...

Le Beau Navire

Je veux te raconter, ô molle enchanteresse!
Les diverses beautés qui parent ta jeunesse;
    Je veux te peindre ta beauté,
Où l'enfance s'allie à la maturité.

Quand tu vas balayant l'air de ta jupe large,
Tu fais l'effet d'un beau vaisseau qui prend le large,
    Chargé de toile, et va roulant
Suivant un rythme doux, et paresseux, et lent.

Sur ton cou large et rond, sur tes épaules grasses,
Ta tête se pavane avec d'étranges grâces;
    D'un air placide et triomphant
Tu passes ton chemin, majestueuse enfant.

Je veux te raconter, ô molle enchanteresse!
Les diverses beautés qui parent ta jeunesse;
    Je veux te peindre ta beauté,
Où l'enfance s'allie à la maturité.

Ta gorge qui s'avance et qui pousse la moire,
Ta gorge triomphante est une belle armoire
    Dont les panneaux bombés et clairs
Comme les boucliers accrochent des éclairs;

Boucliers provoquants, armés de pointes roses!
Armoire à doux secrets, pleine de bonnes choses,
    De vins, de parfums, de liqueurs
Qui feraient délirer les cerveaux et les cœurs!

Quand tu vas balayant l'air de ta jupe large,
Tu fais l'effet d'un beau vaisseau qui prend le large,
    Chargé de toile, et va roulant
Suivant un rythme doux, et paresseux, et lent.

The Beautiful Ship

I would recount for you the charms, allures,
And loveliness that crown that youth of yours,
    O gentle, sweet enchantress mine,
Where tender years and womanhood combine.

Wide skirt aswirl, sweeping the air, you seem
Like some fine ship, sheets to the wind, each beam
    Laden with sail, that glides apace
With lazy, easy roll and languid grace.

Your head, in curious comeliness, stands jutting,
Cocked, from your ample neck and shoulders, strutting
    Proudly, child sure of victory,
As you pass by in tranquil majesty.

I would recount for you the charms, allures,
And loveliness that crown that youth of yours,
    O gentle, sweet enchantress mine,
Where tender years and womanhood combine.

Opal-like shimmers glint your jaunty breast;
Your breast triumphant, like a treasure chest
    Whose bulging panels brave the crash,
Like shields, of thunderbolt and lightning flash.

Pink-pointed shields, defiant in their pose;
Treasure chest filled with wondrous secrets: those
    Liqueurs, wines, scents that would excite
The head and soul to raptures of delight.

Wide skirt aswirl, sweeping the air, you seem
Like some fine ship, sheets to the wind, each beam
    Laden with sail, that glides apace
With lazy, easy roll and languid grace.

Tes nobles jambes, sous les volants qu'elles chassent,
Tourmentent les désirs obscurs et les agacent,
        Comme deux sorcières qui font
Tourner un philtre noir dans un vase profond.

Tes bras, qui se joueraient des précoces hercules,
Sont des boas luisants les solides émules,
        Faits pour serrer obstinément,
Comme pour l'imprimer dans ton cœur, ton amant.

Sur ton cou large et rond, sur tes épaules grasses,
Ta tête se pavane avec d'étranges grâces;
        D'un air placide et triomphant
Tu passes ton chemin, majestueuse enfant.

Your splendid legs, ringed round in furbelow
And flounce, stir passions dark and vague, as though
        They were a pair of witches, who
Churn in their cauldron some black magic brew.

Your arms, which flout young stalwarts' strength, would be
Sleek boas' rivals, fashioned purposely
        To clasp your lover—coiled, entwined—
Ever impressed upon your heart and mind.

Your head, in curious comeliness, stands jutting,
Cocked, from your ample neck and shoulders, strutting
        Proudly, child sure of victory,
As you pass by in tranquil majesty.

L'Invitation au voyage

Mon enfant, ma sœur,
Songe à la douceur
D'aller là-bas vivre ensemble!
Aimer à loisir,
Aimer et mourir
Au pays qui te ressemble!
Les soleils mouillés
De ces ciels brouillés
Pour mon esprit ont les charmes
Si mystérieux
De tes traîtres yeux,
Brillant à travers leurs larmes.

Là, tout n'est qu'ordre et beauté,
Luxe, calme et volupté.

Des meubles luisants,
Polis par les ans,
Décoreraient notre chambre:
Les plus rares fleurs
Mêlant leurs odeurs
Aux vagues senteurs de l'ambre,
Les riches plafonds,
Les miroirs profonds,
La splendeur orientale,
Tout y parlerait
A l'âme en secret
Sa douce langue natale.

Là, tout n'est qu'ordre et beauté,
Luxe, calme et volupté.

Invitation to the Voyage

Imagine, *ma petite,*
Dear sister mine, how sweet
Were we to go and take our pleasure—
Leisurely, you and I—
To live, to love, to die
Off in that land made to your measure!
A land whose suns' moist rays,
Through the skies' misty haze,
Hold quite the same dark charms for me
As do your scheming eyes
When they, in their like wise,
Shine through your tears, perfidiously.

There all is order, naught amiss:
Comfort and beauty, calm and bliss.

Treasure galore—ornate,
Time-glossed—would decorate
Our chamber, where the rarest blooms
Would blend their lavish scent,
Heady and opulent,
With wisps of amber-like perfumes;
Where all the Orient's
Splendid, rich ornaments—
Deep mirrors, ceilings fine—would each,
In confidential tone,
Speak to the soul alone
In its own sweet and secret speech.

There all is order, naught amiss:
Comfort and beauty, calm and bliss.

Vois sur ces canaux
Dormir ces vaisseaux
Dont l'humeur est vagabonde;
C'est pour assouvir
Ton moindre désir
Qu'ils viennent du bout du monde.
—Les soleils couchants
Revêtent les champs,
Les canaux, la ville entière,
D'hyacinthe et d'or;
Le monde s'endort
Dans une chaude lumière.

Là, tout n'est qu'ordre et beauté,
Luxe, calme et volupté.

See how the ships, asleep—
        They who would ply the deep!—
Line the canals: to satisfy
        Your merest whim they come
        From far-flung heathendom
And skim the seven seas. —On high,
        The sunset's rays enfold
        In hyacinth and gold,
Field and canal; and, with the night,
        As shadows gently fall,
        Behold! Life sleeps, and all
Lies bathed in warmth and evening light.

There all is order, naught amiss:
Comfort and beauty, calm and bliss.

Causerie

Vous êtes un beau ciel d'automne, clair et rose!
Mais la tristesse en moi monte comme la mer,
Et laisse, en refluant, sur ma lèvre morose
Le souvenir cuisant de son limon amer.

—Ta main se glisse en vain sur mon sein qui se pâme;
Ce qu'elle cherche, amie, est un lieu saccagé
Par la griffe et la dent féroce de la femme.
Ne cherchez plus mon cœur; les bêtes l'ont mangé.

Mon cœur est un palais flétri par la cohue;
On s'y soûle, on s'y tue, on s'y prend aux cheveux!
—Un parfum nage autour de votre gorge nue!...

O Beauté, dur fléau des âmes, tu le veux!
Avec tes yeux de feu, brillants comme des fêtes,
Calcine ce lambeaux qu'ont épargnés les bêtes!

Chat

You are an autumn sky, all pink and clear!
But sadness wells up in me like the sea;
And, ebbing, leaves upon my lips—dull, drear—
The bitter, biting silt of memory.

—In vain my bosom feels your touch, caressed;
The heart you seek is now no more a heart:
Woman has rent it from my swooning breast;
Devouring beasts have ripped, clawed it apart.

My heart is like a palace, throng-attacked,
By scufflers, drunkards, killers chaos-racked!
—A sweet perfume clings to your bosom bared!...

O Beauty, scourge of souls, you want it still!
With radiant revel-gaze, flame, burn, until
Your eyes consume the scraps my beasts have spared!

A une dame créole

Au pays parfumé que le soleil caresse,
J'ai connu, sous un dais d'arbres tout empourprés
Et de palmiers d'où pleut sur les yeux la paresse,
Une dame créole aux charmes ignorés.

Son teint est pâle et chaud; la brune enchanteresse
A dans le cou des airs noblement maniérés;
Grande et svelte en marchant comme une chasseresse,
Son sourire est tranquille et ses yeux assurés.

Si vous alliez, Madame, au vrai pays de gloire,
Sur les bords de la Seine ou de la verte Loire,
Belle digne d'orner les antiques manoirs,

Vous feriez, à l'abri des ombreuses retraites,
Germer mille sonnets dans le cœur des poëtes,
Que vos grands yeux rendraient plus soumis que vos noirs.

For a Creole Lady

Dawdling in crimsoned arbor's lush recess,
In country sweet-perfumed and sun-caressed—
Fronds dripping eyefuls of pure idleness—
I've known a Creole lady, beauty-blest,

Of charms unsung. Alluring sorceress,
Svelte huntress, lithe of neck and chestnut-tressed;
Pale, warm her hue; mannered her politesse;
Stately her gait; her gaze, smile, self-possessed.

Belle fit to grace our finest old châteaux!
Ah! If, Madame, off in that land of splendor,
You were to loll by verdant banks, where flow

The Seine, the Loire, then would your eyes engender
Sonnets galore, by poets of penned amours,
Rendered more docile than those blacks of yours.

Mœsta et errabunda

Dis-moi, ton cœur, parfois, s'envole-t-il, Agathe,
Loin du noir océan de l'immonde cité,
Vers un autre océan où la splendeur éclate,
Bleu, clair, profond, ainsi que la virginité?
Dis-moi, ton cœur, parfois, s'envole-t-il, Agathe?

La mer, la vaste mer, console nos labeurs!
Quel démon a doté la mer, rauque chanteuse
Qu'accompagne l'immense orgue des vents grondeurs,
De cette fonction sublime de berceuse?
La mer, la vaste mer, console nos labeurs!

Emporte-moi, wagon! enlève-moi, frégate!
Loin! loin! ici la boue est faite de nos pleurs!
—Est-il vrai que parfois le triste cœur d'Agathe
Dise: Loin des remords, des crimes, des douleurs,
Emporte-moi, wagon! enlève-moi, frégate?

Comme vous êtes loin, paradis parfumé,
Où sous un clair azur tout n'est qu'amour et joie,
Où tout ce que l'on aime est digne d'être aimé!
Où dans la volupté pure le cœur se noie!
Comme vous êtes loin, paradis parfumé!

Mais le vert paradis des amours enfantines,
Les courses, les chansons, les baisers, les bouquets,
Les violons vibrant derrière les collines,
Avec les brocs de vin, le soir, dans les bosquets,
—Mais le vert paradis des amours enfantines,

L'innocent paradis, plein de plaisirs furtifs,
Est-il déjà plus loin que l'Inde et que la Chine?
Peut-on le rappeler avec des cris plaintifs,
Et l'animer encor d'une voix argentine,
L'innocent paradis plein de plaisirs furtifs?

Mœsta et errabunda

Tell me, Agathe...Your heart? Does it take flight
From city squalor—ocean dark, despoiled—
Off to another ocean, bursting bright—
Deep, limpid blue—as virgin chaste, unsoiled?
Tell me, Agathe...Your heart? Does it take flight?

The sea, the boundless sea, soothes our travail!
What demon turns its moaning raucous cry,
Over the organ-roar of groaning gale,
Into a lofty, heavenly lullaby?
The sea, the boundless sea, soothes our travail!

Coach, sweep me off! Ship, spirit me away!
Far, far! Our tears bestrew these sodden climes.
—What? My Agathe's sad heart, at times, will say:
"Far from remorse, from woes, and pains, and crimes,
Coach, sweep me off! Ship, spirit me away"?

How distant now, you fragrant paradise,
Where love and joy alone light azure sky,
Where all one loves is worth love's tender price,
Where, steeped in blissfulness, hearts raptured lie!
How distant now, you fragrant paradise!

That paradise of childhood love-delights:
Songs, chases, artless kisses, jugs of wine,
Violins throbbing in the flower-filled nights,
Behind the hills, midst verdant tree and vine...
That paradise of childhood love-delights,

Innocent paradise of furtive pleasure!
What? Flown beyond the Indies? China's shore?
Will plaintive cries call back its simple treasure,
Breathe life into its silvered voice once more,
Innocent paradise of furtive pleasure?

Des baisers froids comme la lune

Le Revenant

Comme les anges à l'œil fauve,
Je reviendrai dans ton alcôve
Et vers toi glisserai sans bruit
Avec les ombres de la nuit;

Et je te donnerai, ma brune,
Des baisers froids comme la lune
Et des caresses de serpent
Autour d'une fosse rampant.

Quand viendra le matin livide,
Tu trouveras ma place vide,
Où jusqu'au soir il fera froid.

Comme d'autres par la tendresse,
Sur ta vie et sur ta jeunesse,
Moi, je veux régner par l'effroi.

The Incubus

Like angels bestial-eyed shall I
Come to your chamber by and by,
And bed beside you, but without
A sound, as night shades draw about.

There shall I give you, dark-skinned love,
Kisses cold as the moon above;
Embrace tight as a snake's, a-slither
Over the grave-pit, hither, thither.

But when the bleak, dull light of dawn
Breaks dim, then will you find me gone;
And cold your bed, till comes the night.

Others may rule your youth, your life,
With tenderness, all sweetness-rife:
I choose to rule you, love, with fright.

Sonnet d'automne

Ils me disent, tes yeux, clairs comme le cristal:
"Pour toi, bizarre amant, quel est donc mon mérite?"
—Sois charmante et tais-toi! Mon cœur, que tout irrite,
Excepté la candeur de l'antique animal,

Ne veut pas te montrer son secret infernal,
Berceuse dont la main aux longs sommeils m'invite,
Ni sa noire légende avec la flamme écrite.
Je hais la passion et l'esprit me fait mal!

Aimons-nous doucement. L'Amour dans sa guérite,
Ténébreux, embusqué, bande son arc fatal.
Je connais les engins de son vieil arsenal:

Crime, horreur et folie!—O pâle marguerite!
Comme moi n'es-tu pas un soleil automnal,
O ma si blanche, ô ma si froide Marguerite?

Autumn Sonnet

I look into your crystal eyes and see:
"Why me, strange lover? What am I, to meet
With your esteem?" Hush, and play coy, my sweet!
My heart, at odds, save with the brutal, free

Lusts of the flesh, must hide its damned ennui;
Hide, too, its black, flame-written lore, discreet.
Lull me to slumbers deep, with leisured beat:
I've done with passion, and I loathe esprit.

Let's gently love. Eros, in his retreat
Ensconced, pulls taut his death-bow, furtively.
I know too well his ancient weaponry:

Crime, folly, fright... White-petaled marguerite,
Aren't you condemned, like autumn sun, to be—
My other Marguerite!—pale, cold, like me?

Tristesses de la lune

Ce soir, la lune rêve avec plus de paresse;
Ainsi qu'une beauté, sur de nombreux coussins,
Qui d'une main distraite et légère caresse
Avant de s'endormir le contour de ses seins,

Sur le dos satiné des molles avalanches,
Mourante, elle se livre aux longues pâmoisons,
Et promène ses yeux sur les visions blanches
Qui montent dans l'azur comme des floraisons.

Quand parfois sur ce globe, en sa langueur oisive,
Elle laisse filer une larme furtive,
Un poëte pieux, ennemi du sommeil,

Dans le creux de sa main prend cette larme pâle,
Aux reflets irisés comme un fragment d'opale,
Et la met dans son cœur loin des yeux du soleil.

Sorrows of the Moon

Languid, tonight, the moon's calm reverie;
And, like a beauty who, encushioned, rests,
Waiting for sleep, and lightly, lovingly
Fondles the fullness of her ample breasts,

On satin avalanches softly lying,
She swoons enraptured, peers at visions white
That rise up like bouquets as she lies dying,
Flowering in the azure of the night.

And, languorous, when she lets a furtive tear
At times come falling to this earthly sphere,
A pious poet, enemy of sleep,

Cups in his palm that pale tear, like a bit
Of iridescent opal, keeping it
Far from the sun's eyes, hidden bosom-deep.

Les Chats

Les amoureux fervents et les savants austères
Aiment également, dans leur mûre saison,
Les chats puissants et doux, orgueil de la maison,
Qui comme eux sont frileux et comme eux sédentaires.

Amis de la science et de la volupté,
Ils cherchent le silence et l'horreur des ténèbres;
L'Erèbe les eût pris pour ses coursiers funèbres,
S'ils pouvaient au servage incliner leur fierté.

Ils prennent en songeant les nobles attitudes
Des grands sphinx allongés au fond des solitudes,
Qui semblent s'endormir dans un rêve sans fin;

Leurs reins féconds sont pleins d'étincelles magiques,
Et des parcelles d'or, ainsi qu'un sable fin,
Etoilent vaguement leurs prunelles mystiques.

Cats

Hot-blooded lovers, in their latter days,
And scholars stern of mien, dote upon cats,
Those lordly, lithe household aristocrats:
Like them, thin-skinned; like them, set in their ways.

Passionate and astute, randy and wise,
Craving the hushed, portentous gloom, they might
Have served as couriers in the Stygian night
Had they but deigned assume a servile guise.

Like sphinxes in some lonely waste, that seem
Dozing forever in an endless dream,
Musing, they sprawl, striking that pose august:

Their rich flanks bristle with a magic glimmer;
Glistening sparks and flecks of gilt beshimmer,
Dimly, their mystic eyes, with golden dust.

Les hiboux se tiennent rangés,

Ainsi que des dieux étrangers

Les Hiboux

Sous les ifs noirs qui les abritent,
Les hiboux se tiennent rangés,
Ainsi que des dieux étrangers,
Dardant leur œil rouge. Ils méditent.

Sans remuer ils se tiendront
Jusqu'à l'heure mélancolique
Où, poussant le soleil oblique,
Les ténèbres s'établiront.

Leur attitude au sage enseigne
Qu'il faut en ce monde qu'il craigne
Le tumulte et le mouvement;

L'homme ivre d'une ombre qui passe
Porte toujours le châtiment
D'avoir voulu changer de place.

The Owls

Beneath the black and sheltering yews,
Darting their glance with sharp red eyes,
The owls align in ordered wise
Like alien gods. And there they muse.

Thus will they perch, stock-still, each one,
Until night's somber shades begin—
Drear and morose—to settle in,
Pushing away the slant-rayed sun.

Their mien should prove to Man the sense
Of fighting shy of turbulence
And movement in this life. Because,

Drunk on a passing shadow, he
Will always pay a penalty
For not remaining where he was.

La Pipe

Je suis la pipe d'un auteur;
On voit, à contempler ma mine
D'Abyssinienne ou de Cafrine,
Que mon maître est un grand fumeur.

Quand il est comblé de douleur,
Je fume comme la chaumine
Où se prépare la cuisine
Pour le retour du laboureur.

J'enlace et je berce son âme
Dans le réseau mobile et bleu
Qui monte de ma bouche en feu,

Et je roule un puissant dictame
Qui charme son cœur et guérit
De ses fatigues son esprit.

The Pipe

I am an author's pipe. It's clear,
To see my face—like some Kaffir
Or Ethiope, dark-hued—that he
Spends many an hour smoking me.

When he sits, bowed with grief and woe,
I smoke like country bungalow,
Where, in the kitchen, steaming hot,
Awaits the ploughman's supper-pot.

I lull his soul in my embrace
Of blue-gray wisps, rising in space
Out of my fiery mouth; and wind

Him round in balm-like blandishment,
Charming his weary heart, content
To soothe his spirit, calm his mind.

La Musique

La musique souvent me prend comme une mer!
      Vers ma pâle étoile,
Sous un plafond de brume ou dans un vaste éther,
      Je mets à la voile;

La poitrine en avant et les poumons gonflés
      Comme de la toile,
J'escalade le dos des flots amoncelés
      Que la nuit me voile;

Je sens vibrer en moi toutes les passions
      D'un vaisseau qui souffre;
Le bon vent, la tempête et ses convulsions

      Sur l'immense gouffre
Me bercent. D'autres fois, calme plat, grand miroir
      De mon désespoir!

Music

Often, music engulfs me like a sea;
          I set my course, afar,
Mist-canopied, through vast infinity,
            Toward my dim, distant star;

Proud-bosomed, at the bar I stand, upright,
           Lungs puffed like panoply
Of sails, and ride the swelling waves that night
          Veils and conceals from me;

I feel within me all the quivering woes
          Born to a vessel's soul:
Over the deep abyss, when tempest blows

         Or breeze wafts mild, I roll,
I pitch... Or when the sea's calm, glassy air
        Mirrors my own despair!

Sépulture

Si par une nuit lourde et sombre
Un bon chrétien, par charité,
Derrière quelque vieux décombre
Enterre votre corps vanté,

A l'heure où les chastes étoiles
Ferment leurs yeux appesantis,
L'araignée y fera ses toiles,
Et la vipère ses petits;

Vous entendrez toute l'année
Sur votre tête condamnée
Les cris lamentables des loups

Et des sorcières faméliques,
Les ébats des vieillards lubriques
Et les complots des noirs filous.

Burial

Perhaps one sultry, somber night,
Behind some hovel—crumbling, old—
A tenderhearted Christian might
Bury your body, late extolled.

Then will the taintless stars begin
To close tired eyes; a-crawl among
Your last remains, spider will spin
Her web, and viper spawn her young.

Year out, year in, over your head
Entombed, will sound the doleful, dread
Howl of the wolves; screech of the foul,

Rattleboned witches; and the sprees
Of hoary graybeard debauchees,
And schemes of black-souled thugs a-prowl.

Sans éperons, sans fouet, il essouffle un cheval,

Fantôme comme lui, rosse apocalyptique

Une Gravure fantastique

Ce spectre singulier n'a pour toute toilette,
Grotesquement campé sur son front de squelette,
Qu'un diadème affreux sentant le carnaval.
Sans éperons, sans fouet, il essouffle un cheval,
Fantôme comme lui, rosse apocalyptique,
Qui bave des naseaux comme un épileptique.
Au travers de l'espace ils s'enfoncent tous deux,
Et foulent l'infini d'un sabot hasardeux.
Le cavalier promène un sabre qui flamboie
Sur les foules sans nom que sa monture broie,
Et parcourt, comme un prince inspectant sa maison,
Le cimetière immense et froid, sans horizon,
Où gisent, aux lueurs d'un soleil blanc et terne,
Les peuples de l'histoire ancienne et moderne.

A Fantastic Engraving

Skull decked, askew, with tawdry diadem
Carnivalesque—no other frill, no gem,
No garment: nothing, not the merest rag—
This ghastly skeleton, bone-bare, on ghostly nag,
Gallops through space. No spurs, no whips...
And yet his steed pants toward Apocalypse,
Nostrils a-snort in epileptic fit.
Headlong they rush, athwart the infinite,
With rash and trampling hoof. The cavalier,
His flashing sword aflame, slashes—now here,
Now there—amongst the nameless slaughtered horde;
Then goes inspecting, like some manor-lord,
The charnel-ground, chill and unbounded, where,
Under a bleak sun's pallid, leaden glare,
History's great sepulchered masses lie,
From ages near and ages long gone by.

La Cloche fêlée

Il est amer et doux, pendant les nuits d'hiver,
D'écouter, près du feu qui palpite et qui fume,
Les souvenirs lointains lentement s'élever
Au bruit des carillons qui chantent dans la brume.

Bienheureuse la cloche au gosier vigoureux
Qui, malgré sa vieillesse, alerte et bien portante,
Jette fidèlement son cri religieux,
Ainsi qu'un vieux soldat qui veille sous la tente!

Moi, mon âme et fêlée, et lorsqu'en ses ennuis
Elle veut de ses chants peupler l'air froid des nuits,
Il arrive souvent que sa voix affaiblie

Semble le râle épais d'un blessé qu'on oublie
Au bord d'un lac de sang, sous un grand tas de morts,
Et qui meurt, sans bouger, dans d'immenses efforts.

The Cracked Bell

How bittersweet it is, on winter's night,
To listen, by the sputtering, smoking fire,
As distant memories, through the fog-dimmed light,
Rise, to the muffled chime of churchbell choir.

Lucky the bell—still full and deep of throat,
Clear-voiced despite its years, strong, eloquent—
That rings, with faithful tongue, its pious note
Like an old soldier, wakeful, in his tent!

My soul lies cracked; and when, in its despair,
Pealing, it tries to fill the cold night air
With its lament, it often sounds, instead,

Like some poor wounded wretch—long left for dead
Beneath a pile of corpses, lying massed
By bloody pool—rattling, gasping his last.

Le beau valet de cœur et la dame de pique

Causent sinistrement de leurs amours défunts

Spleen

Pluviôse, irrité contre la ville entière,
De son urne à grands flots verse un froid ténébreux
Aux pâles habitants du voisin cimetière
Et la mortalité sur les faubourgs brumeux.

Mon chat sur le carreau cherchant une litière
Agite sans repos son corps maigre et galeux;
L'âme d'un vieux poëte erre dans la gouttière
Avec la triste voix d'un fantôme frileux.

Le bourdon se lamente, et la bûche enfumée
Accompagne en fausset la pendule enrhumée,
Cependant qu'en un jeu plein de sales parfums,

Héritage fatal d'une vieille hydropique,
Le beau valet de cœur et la dame de pique
Causent sinistrement de leurs amours défunts.

Spleen

Vexed at the city, bleak, damp Pluviôse
Empties his urn's foreboding chill; and while
Death rains on drear faubourgs, he soddens those
Pale shades who dwell in graveyard domicile.

Seeking a place to squat, my cat comes, goes—
Poor scurvy, scrawny beast—asprawl the tile;
Under the eaves, sad, soulful tremolos
Echo a phantom poet's cold exile.

The smoking log crackles its crisp staccato
Over the rusty clock's hoarse ostinato.
Doleful the drone; while in their perfume-worn

Old pack, left by some now-dead dropsied crone,
Fair Jack of Hearts and Queen of Spades bemoan
In sullen colloquy their loves forlorn.

Spleen

J'ai plus de souvenirs que si j'avais mille ans.

Un gros meuble à tiroirs encombré de bilans,
De vers, de billets doux, de procès, de romances,
Avec de lourds cheveux roulés dans des quittances,
Cache moins de secrets que mon triste cerveau.
C'est une pyramide, un immense caveau,
Qui contient plus de morts que la fosse commune.
—Je suis un cimetière abhorré de la lune,
Où, comme des remords, se traînent de longs vers
Qui s'acharnent toujours sur mes morts les plus chers.
Je suis un vieux boudoir plein de roses fanées,
Où gît tout un fouillis de modes surannées,
Où les pastels plaintifs et les pâles Boucher,
Seuls, respirent l'odeur d'un flacon débouché.

Rien n'égale en longueur les boiteuses journées,
Quand sous les lourds flocons des neigeuses années
L'ennui, fruit de la morne incuriosité,
Prend les proportions de l'immortalité.
—Désormais tu n'es plus, ô matière vivante!
Qu'un granit entouré d'une vague épouvante,
Assoupi dans le fond d'un Saharah brumeux;
Un vieux sphinx ignoré du monde insoucieux,
Oublié sur la carte, et dont l'humeur farouche
Ne chante qu'aux rayons du soleil qui se couche.

Spleen

More memories, mine, than from a thousand years.

One of those huge and cluttered chiffoniers—
Drawers stuffed with verses, lawsuits, balance sheets,
Love letters, locks of hair rolled in receipts—
Hides fewer secrets than my woeful brain.
Vast cavern, pyramid... Its walls contain
More corpses than the paupers' burial ditch.
I am a graveyard, moon-abhorred, in which,
Like litany of dolorous regret,
Long worms, in slithering crawl, aswarm, beset
My dearest dead. An old boudoir am I,
Strewn round with faded roses, and where lie
Yesteryear's bygone fashions; where, pell-mell,
Pallid Bouchers and many a sad pastel
Are left, abandoned and alone, to quaff
The lingering scent from an uncorked carafe.

Nothing can match those endless, crippled days
When, blizzard-blown, chill winter overlays
Ennui with heavy snows: drear apathy,
Taking the shape of immortality.
—Henceforth, O living flesh, you are a mere
Granitic mass, enwrapped in some vague fear,
Drowsing on some Sahara's distant sand,
Like an old sphinx, unmapped, in some lost land;
And whose splenetic humors, through the haze,
Sing only to the sunset's dying rays.

Spleen

Je suis comme le roi d'un pays pluvieux,
Riche, mais impuissant, jeune et pourtant très vieux,
Qui, de ses précepteurs méprisant les courbettes,
S'ennuie avec ses chiens comme avec d'autres bêtes.
Rien ne peut l'égayer, ni gibier, ni faucon,
Ni son peuple mourant en face du balcon.
Du bouffon favori la grotesque ballade
Ne distrait plus le front de ce cruel malade;
Son lit fleurdelisé se transforme en tombeau,
Et les dames d'atour, pour qui tout prince est beau,
Ne savent plus trouver d'impudique toilette
Pour tirer un souris de ce jeune squelette.
Le savant qui lui fait de l'or n'a jamais pu
De son être extirper l'élément corrompu,
Et dans ces bains de sang qui des Romains nous viennent,
Et dont sur leurs vieux jours les puissants se souviennent,
Il n'a su réchauffer ce cadavre hébété
Où coule au lieu de sang l'eau verte du Léthé.

Spleen

I'm like the king of some dank land—wet, cold—
Rich and yet powerless, young and yet old,
Who spurns his tutors' toadying posturings,
Bored with his hounds and with all living things.
Naught cheers him: neither hunt nor falcon's flight,
Nor even, from his balcony, the sight
Of subjects dying. And, no matter how
His fool would soothe the tyrant's feverish brow
With ribald ditty, all in vain! His bed,
Blazoned with fleur-de-lis, becomes instead
A very tomb. The tiring-dames—the kind
Who think all princes fair!—despair to find
Dress indiscreet enough to draw a smile
From this young skeleton. And all the while
His alchemist-physician does his best—
But fails—to exorcise the royal breast
Of its malaise. Those Roman bloodbaths, too,
No longer do what once they used to do—
What aged potentates recall they did—
To cure our mind-benighted invalid:
To warm to life that corpse, soul-stupefied,
Where flows not blood, but Lethe's brackish tide.

Spleen

Quand le ciel bas et lourd pèse comme un couvercle
Sur l'esprit gémissant en proie aux longs ennuis,
Et que de l'horizon embrassant tout le cercle
Il nous verse un jour noir plus triste que les nuits;

Quand la terre est changée en un cachot humide,
Où l'Espérance, comme une chauve-souris,
S'en va battant les murs de son aile timide
Et se cognant la tête à des plafonds pourris;

Quand la pluie étalant ses immenses traînées
D'une vaste prison imite les barreaux,
Et qu'un peuple muet d'infâmes araignées
Vient tendre ses filets au fond de nos cerveaux,

Des cloches tout à coup sautent avec furie
Et lancent vers le ciel un affreux hurlement,
Ainsi que des esprits errants et sans patrie
Qui se mettent à geindre opiniâtrement.

—Et de longs corbillards, sans tambours ni musique,
Défilent lentement dans mon âme; l'Espoir,
Vaincu, pleure, et l'Angoisse atroce, despotique,
Sur mon crâne incliné plante son drapeau noir.

Spleen

When, on our groaning, ennui-ridden soul,
The heavens hang low, weigh like a lid, pressed tight;
When, circling the horizon like a bowl,
They pour a daylight sad as blackest night;

When earth turns dungeon dank, where Hope, much like
A bat, entrapped, in desperation seems
To flail the walls with timid wing, and strike
Her head against the ceiling's rotting beams;

When cloudbursts rend the air and, roundabout,
Form a vast prison cell with bars of rain;
And when a host of spiders, mute, set out
To weave their loathsome webs deep in our brain;

Then, all at once, wild bells leap to the fore
And hurl a frightful clamor at the sky,
Like spirits, wandering homeless, that deplore
Their grievous fate with endless, doleful cry.

—And in my soul hearses proceed apace—
No drums, no fanfare—long their march and slow;
Hope, beaten, weeps; and Woe, brash tyrant base,
Plants his black pennant in my skull, bowed low.

Obsession

Grands bois, vous m'effrayez comme des cathédrales;
Vous hurlez comme l'orgue; et dans nos cœurs maudits,
Chambres d'éternel deuil où vibrent de vieux râles,
Répondent les échos de vos *De profundis*.

Je te hais, Océan! tes bonds et tes tumultes,
Mon esprit les retrouve en lui; ce rire amer
De l'homme vaincu, plein de sanglots et d'insultes,
Je l'entends dans le rire énorme de la mer.

Comme tu me plairais, ô nuit! sans ces étoiles
Dont la lumière parle un langage connu!
Car je cherche le vide, et le noir, et le nu!

Mais les ténèbres sont elles-mêmes des toiles
Où vivent, jaillissant de mon œil par milliers,
Des êtres disparus aux regards familiers.

Obsession

Like vast cathedrals, woods, you frighten me:
You bellow like an organ's wheezing moan;
Our hearts, accursed, through all eternity,
Echo your *De profundis*, mournful drone.

I loathe you, sea, you of the raging tide:
My soul perceives its double in your swell;
And in your laughter's roar, I hear—sobbed, sighed—
The taunted victim's bitter laugh as well.

Night, I would find you to my taste, were there
No stars to speak their lucid tongue; for I
Yearn for the bleak, the barren: black and bare.

But shade itself becomes a canvas, where
A myriad souls live on, gushed from my eye;
Departed souls, with their familiar air.

Le Goût du néant

Morne esprit, autrefois amoureux de la lutte,
L'Espoir, dont l'éperon attisait ton ardeur,
Ne veut plus t'enfourcher! Couche-toi sans pudeur,
Vieux cheval dont le pied à chaque obstacle butte.

Résigne-toi, mon cœur; dors ton sommeil de brute.

Esprit vaincu, fourbu! Pour toi, vieux maraudeur,
L'amour n'a plus de goût, non plus que la dispute;
Adieu donc, chants du cuivre et soupirs de la flûte!
Plaisirs, ne tentez plus un cœur sombre et boudeur!

Le Printemps adorable a perdu son odeur!

Et le Temps m'engloutit minute par minute,
Comme la neige immense un corps pris de roideur;
Je contemple d'en haut le globe en sa rondeur,
Et je n'y cherche plus l'abri d'une cahute.

Avalanche, veux-tu m'emporter dans ta chute?

The Taste for Nothingness

Dull soul, gone now your thirst for victory!
Hope will not mount you, he whose spurs once pressed
You onward! Go, old nag! Go take your rest,
Poor beast unsure of hoof and weak of knee.

Sleep, loutish heart, and let be what will be.

Spent soul, for you, old rogue, what interest
Could love still have? Or quarrel's obloquy?
Adieu, loud brasses, flutes' suave melody!
Pleasures, tempt not a heart by gloom possessed!

Gone now Spring's fragrance, Nature's loveliest!

Minute by minute Time envelops me
Like blizzard snows, engulfs my frigid breast.
I look down on our globe and seek no nest,
No refuge in its round immensity.

Avalanche, will you come and sweep me free?

Alchimie de la douleur

L'un t'éclaire avec son ardeur,
L'autre en toi met son deuil, Nature!
Ce qui dit à l'un: Sépulture!
Dit à l'autre: Vie et splendeur!

Hermès inconnu qui m'assistes
Et qui toujours m'intimidas,
Tu me rends l'égal de Midas,
Le plus triste des alchimistes;

Par toi je change l'or en fer
Et le paradis en enfer;
Dans le suaire des nuages

Je découvre un cadavre cher,
Et sur les célestes rivages
Je bâtis de grands sarcophages.

Grief's Alchemy

Some magnify you, Nature; some
Condemn you with their every breath.
What one perceives a "Living Death,"
Another deems "Life's Glorydom"!

Ah, Hermes—obscure, fearsome—who
Gave me the touch of Midas: he
Most skilled (and cursed!) in alchemy.
My gold turns iron, thanks to you!

My heaven turns hell! There in the sky
I see a corpse, familiar, lie
Wrapped in a winding-sheet: a shroud

That once I might have thought a cloud.
And on the heavenly shores my eye
Goes building great sarcophagi.

Horreur sympathique

De ce ciel bizarre et livide,
Tourmenté comme ton destin,
Quels pensers dans ton âme vide
Descendent? Réponds, libertin.

—Insatiablement avide
De l'obscur et de l'incertain,
Je ne geindrai pas comme Ovide
Chassé du paradis latin.

Cieux déchirés comme des grèves,
En vous se mire mon orgueil;
Vos vastes nuages en deuil

Sont les corbillards de mes rêves,
En vos lueurs sont le reflet
De l'Enfer où mon cœur se plaît.

Harmony of Horror

That vapid soul of yours... I pray,
Tell me what fancy occupies
Its tortured wastes, my fine roué,
Bare as those odd and ashen skies.

—Only the vague, the dark, the gray
Enthralls my ever lusting eyes:
No whining Ovid, castaway,
Mourning my Roman paradise!

Heavens, like shores ripped by the tide,
You are the mirror of my pride;
Your clouds, in widow's weeds of night,

Conduct the death march of my dreams;
And in your flare and glimmer gleams
The fire of Hell, my soul's delight.

L'Héautontimorouménos

À J.G.F.

Je te frapperai sans colère
Et sans haine, comme un boucher,
Comme Moïse le rocher!
Et je ferai de ta paupière,

Pour abreuver mon Saharah,
Jaillir les eaux de la souffrance.
Mon désir gonflé d'espérance
Sur tes pleurs salés nagera

Comme un vaisseau qui prend le large,
Et dans mon cœur qu'ils soûleront
Tes chers sanglots retentiront
Comme un tambour qui bat la charge!

Ne suis-je pas un faux accord
Dans la divine symphonie,
Grâce à la vorace Ironie
Qui me secoue et qui me mord?

Elle est dans ma voix, la criarde!
C'est tout mon sang, ce poison noir!
Je suis le sinistre miroir
Où la mégère se regarde!

Je suis la plaie et le couteau!
Je suis le soufflet et la joue!
Je suis les membres et la roue,
Et la victime et le bourreau!

Je suis de mon cœur le vampire,
—Un de ces grands abandonnés
Au rire éternel condamnés,
Et qui ne peuvent plus sourire!

Heautontimoroumenos

FOR J.G.F.

Yes, I will strike you; though with no
Rancor, but as a butcher might,
Or Moses, when he went to smite
The rock. And from your eyes will flow

The waters of your agony
Over my parched Sahara's sand;
And my desire, sails filled, and fanned
By hope, will ply your salt-tear sea.

My heart, drunk on your sigh, your sob,
Will echo lovingly, resound
Like drums that sound the charge, and pound
Their rhythm's beat with every throb.

Does not that glutton, Irony,
Who bites and grips and shakes me thus,
Make of me a cacophonous
Note in the heavenly symphony?

Her shriek is mine, my evil twin!
So too her poison blood, alas!
Yes, mine as well! I am the glass
The shrew sees her reflection in!

I am the dagger and the wound!
I am the whip, I am the back!
The neck and noose; the limbs, the rack!
I, the dragooners and dragooned!

I am my heart's own vampire vile!
—One of life's great forlorn, forever
Doomed to an endless laugh, but never
Able to wear the simplest smile!

Paysage

Je veux, pour composer chastement mes églogues,
Coucher auprès du ciel, comme les astrologues,
Et, voisin des clochers, écouter en rêvant
Leurs hymnes solennels emportés par le vent.
Les deux mains au menton, du haut de ma mansarde,
Je verrai l'atelier qui chante et qui bavarde;
Les tuyaux, les clochers, ces mâts de la cité,
Et les grands ciels qui font rêver d'éternité.

Il est doux, à travers les brumes, de voir naître
L'étoile dans l'azur, la lampe à la fenêtre,
Les fleuves de charbon monter au firmament
Et la lune verser son pâle enchantement.
Je verrai les printemps, les étés, les automnes;
Et quand viendra l'hiver aux neiges monotones,
Je fermerai partout portières et volets
Pour bâtir dans la nuit mes féeriques palais.
Alors je rêverai des horizons bleuâtres,
Des jardins, des jets d'eau pleurant dans les albâtres,
Des baisers, des oiseaux chantant soir et matin,
Et tout ce que l'Idylle a de plus enfantin.
L'Emeute, tempêtant vainement à ma vitre,
Ne fera pas lever mon front de mon pupitre;
Car je serai plongé dans cette volupté
D'évoquer le Printemps avec ma volonté,
De tirer un soleil de mon cœur, et de faire
De mes pensers brûlants une tiède atmosphère.

Landscape

To craft my eclogues in chaste, proper wise,
I want to lie, outspread against the skies
Like olden-day astrologers; and muse
Hard by church towers, rising high, and whose
Dour, solemn hymns waft on the wind. Here, in
My garret chamber will I sit, with chin
In hand, gaze at the workshops' much ado;
The chimneys, steeples, reaching to the blue—
Ship masts in city guise—and somberly
Meditate on the heavens' eternity.

How sweet, to pierce the haze and see, afar,
The azure brightened by a newborn star;
The window, by a lamp; to see the swell
Of curling smoke; the pale moon's witching spell.
Here will I watch each summer, spring, and fall;
And when the winters bring squall upon squall,
I shall close all the doors and shutters tight,
And build my fairy castles in the night.
Then will I be transported in my dreams
To blue-horizoned clime, with gardens, streams,
Fine alabaster pools, jets weeping free,
Kisses galore, birds singing endlessly:
All the idyllic childhood joys. In vain
Will Riot bellow, storm my windowpane
To make me raise my head. For I shall keep
Calling my will-wrought Spring to life, plunged deep
In bliss, as from my heart a sunshine bright
Tempers my burning thoughts to warm delight.

Le Soleil

Le long du vieux faubourg, où pendent aux masures
Les persiennes, abri des secrètes luxures,
Quand le soleil cruel frappe à traits redoublés
Sur la ville et les champs, sur les toits et les blés,
Je vais m'exercer seul à ma fantasque escrime,
Flairant dans tous les coins les hasards de la rime,
Trébuchant sur let mots comme sur les pavés,
Heurtant parfois des vers depuis longtemps rêvés.

Ce père nourricier, ennemi des chloroses,
Eveille dans les champs les vers comme les roses;
Il fait s'évaporer les soucis vers le ciel,
Et remplit les cerveaux et les ruches de miel.
C'est lui qui rajeunit les porteurs de béquilles
Et les rend gais et doux comme des jeunes filles,
Et commande aux moissons de croître et de mûrir
Dans le cœur immortel qui toujours veut fleurir!

Quand, ainsi qu'un poëte, il descend dans les villes,
Il ennoblit le sort des choses les plus viles,
Et s'introduit en roi, sans bruit et sans valets,
Dans tous les hôpitaux et dans tous le palais.

The Sun

Often, when beats the sun, pounding away
On city and field—on roofs and crops—I stray
Through distant quarters where slum windows hide
Vile orgies, curtain-veiled, afoot inside;
Alone I go, indulging in my sport,
Fencing—here, there—with rhymes of oddest sort,
Stumbling on cobble-words, stubbing my toe,
At times, on verses dreamed of long ago.

This nurturing father, sun, archest of foes
Of ills anemic, wakes the worm, the rose,
Field-born; sucks dry our cares, honeys the hives,
And fills the brain. Through him the cripple thrives,
Uncrutched, gay as a schoolgirl. He it is
That makes the harvest sprout and grow. And his,
The powerful and everlasting art
To make it flower, immortal, in our heart.

Into the city, poet-like, he brings
A fairer fate to quite the foulest things;
And king—though quiet and unattended—he
Tends hospital and palace equally.

Le Cygne

À VICTOR HUGO

I

Andromaque, je pense à vous! Ce petit fleuve,
Pauvre et triste miroir où jadis resplendit
L'immense majesté de vos douleurs de veuve,
Ce Simoïs menteur qui par vos pleurs grandit,

A fécondé soudain ma mémoire fertile,
Comme je traversais le nouveau Carrousel.
Le vieux Paris n'est plus (la forme d'une ville
Change plus vite, hélas! que le cœur d'un mortel);

Je ne vois qu'en esprit tout ce camp de baraques,
Ces tas de chapiteaux ébauchés et de fûts,
Les herbes, les gros blocs verdis par l'eau des flaques,
Et, brillant aux carreaux, le bric-à-brac confus.

Là s'étalait jadis une ménagerie;
Là je vis, un matin, à l'heure où sous les cieux
Froids et clairs le Travail s'éveille, où la voirie
Pousse un sombre ouragan dans l'air silencieux,

Un cygne qui s'était évadé de sa cage,
Et, de ses pieds palmés frottant le pavé sec,
Sur le sol raboteux traînait son blanc plumage.
Près d'un ruisseau sans eau la bête ouvrant le bec

Baignait nerveusement ses ailes dans la poudre,
Et disait, le cœur plein de son beau lac natal:
"Eau, quand donc pleuvras-tu? quand tonneras-tu, foudre?"
Je vois ce malheureux, mythe étrange et fatal,

Vers le ciel quelquefois, comme l'homme d'Ovide,
Vers le ciel ironique et cruellement bleu,
Sur son cou convulsif tendant sa tête avide,
Comme s'il adressait des reproches à Dieu!

The Swan

FOR VICTOR HUGO

I

I turn my thoughts to you, Andromache.
Bred by that specious brook whose yesteryears
Of widow-woes mirrored your majesty—
That would-be Simois, fed by your tears—

Suddenly, crossing the new Carrousel,
My fertile mind conceived your counterpart.
Old Paris is no more. (Ah, truth to tell,
Cities change faster than the human heart!)

Only my mind's eye sees what was: that vast
Hovel-filled field, shafts, cornices a-tumble,
Weeds, great blocks puddled green with moss, amassed
Mid glassed panes shimmering their rubble jumble.

There a menagerie once stood; and there,
One morning, in that cold, clear hour of dawn,
When Work awakes and dustmen churn the air,
Stirring their silent squalls, I saw a swan,

Freed from his cage somehow; his great webbed feet
Clawing the arid ground, he dragged his tail,
White-plumed, about the craggy, cobbled street,
Trying, with beak agape—to no avail—

To bathe his fluttering wings in what had been
A stream, now only dust; and, in his pain,
Dreamed of his native lake, moaned his chagrin:
"O storm! Where, now, your thunder and your rain?"

I see that poor beast still, myth marked for death,
Neck taut, like Ovid's Man, stretched toward a sky
Of harsh, sardonic blue; each panting breath
Seeming a stern rebuke to God on high!

161

II

Paris change! mais rien dans ma mélancolie
N'a bougé! palais neufs, échafaudages, blocs,
Vieux faubourgs, tout pour moi devient allégorie,
Et mes chers souvenirs sont plus lourds que des rocs.

Aussi devant ce Louvre une image m'opprime:
Je pense à mon grand cygne, avec ses gestes fous,
Comme les exilés, ridicule et sublime,
Et rongé d'un désir sans trêve! et puis à vous,

Andromaque, des bras d'un grand époux tombée,
Vil bétail, sous la main du superbe Pyrrhus,
Auprès d'un tombeau vide en extase courbée;
Veuve d'Hector, hélas! et femme d'Hélénus!

Je pense à la négresse, amaigrie et phthisique,
Piétinant dans la boue, et cherchant, l'œil hagard,
Les cocotiers absents de la superbe Afrique
Derrière la muraille immense du brouillard;

A quiconque a perdu ce qui ne se retrouve
Jamais, jamais! à ceux qui s'abreuvent de pleurs
Et tettent la Douleur comme une bonne louve!
Aux maigres orphelins séchant comme des fleurs!

Ainsi dans la forêt où mon esprit s'exile
Un vieux Souvenir sonne à plein souffle du cor!
Je pense aux matelots oubliés dans une île,
Aux captifs, aux vaincus!... à bien d'autres encor!

II

Yes, Paris changes! But my wistful woe
Remains! For me, all becomes metaphor:
Faubourg and palace—old, new—come and go;
Weighty, my memories of what is no more.

And so, here by the Louvre, my thoughts, obsessed,
Turn to my swan of flailing wing, and who,
Like exiles—lordliest and lowliest—
Yearns with an endless grief; and then to you,

Chatteled Andromache—proud Pyrrhos' slave,
Rent from a hero's bed—wailing your loss,
Bowed low, alas, beside an empty grave:
You, Hector's widow, wife to Helenos!

My thoughts turn to the negress, wasting, wan,
Slogging through mud amid the mist and frost,
Who, wild-eyed, longs for Africa, long gone,
And stately coco-palms, now ever lost;

To those now and forevermore bereft!
Those who suck Sorrow's teat, she-wolf benign,
Midst showers of tears! Those wizened orphans left,
Like faded flowers, to wither on the vine!

In forest exile thus—my soul's grim lot—
Memory's horn echoes its blaring brass!
I think of seamen, long marooned, forgot;
Castaways, slaves... and many more, alas!

"Je n'ai pas oublié, voisine de la ville... "

Je n'ai pas oublié, voisine de la ville,
Notre blanche maison, petite mais tranquille;
Sa Pomone de plâtre et sa vieille Vénus
Dans un bosquet chétif cachant leurs membres nus,
Et le soleil, le soir, ruisselant et superbe,
Qui, derrière la vitre où se brisait sa gerbe,
Semblait, grand œil ouvert dans le ciel curieux,
Contempler nos dîners longs et silencieux,
Répandant largement ses beaux reflets de cierge
Sur la nappe frugale et les rideaux de serge.

"I still recall our little house, out there... "

I still recall our little house, out there
Beyond the town, white-painted, with its air
Of calm; and in the patch of greenery,
Trying to hide their plaster nudity,
Pomona and an aging Venus; and,
Streaming, the setting sun, haughty and grand,
Rays breaking on our window, like an eye,
Peering upon us from a curious sky,
And that, flickering taper-like, would cast
Its glints on many a silent, long repast;
On frugal table, set without a frill;
On curtains woven of the plainest twill.

Brumes et pluies

O fins d'automne, hivers, printemps trempés de boue,
Endormeuses saisons! je vous aime et vous loue
D'envelopper ainsi mon cœur et mon cerveau
D'un linceul vaporeux et d'un vague tombeau.

Dans cette grande plaine où l'autan froid se joue,
Où par les longues nuits la girouette s'enroue,
Mon âme mieux qu'au temps du tiède renouveau
Ouvrira largement ses ailes de corbeau.

Rien n'est plus doux au cœur plein de choses funèbres,
Et sur qui dès longtemps descendent les frimas,
O blafardes saisons, reines de nos climats,

Que l'aspect permanent de vos pâles ténèbres,
—Si ce n'est, par un soir sans lune, deux à deux,
D'endormir la douleur sur un lit hasardeux.

Mists and Rains

O waning autumn, winter, mud-soaked spring,
Seasons of sleep! I love you, and I sing
Your praises; for your clouds enfold, enwomb
My heart and mind in shrouds of mist, dim tomb.

In your long wind-chilled nightscape, clangoring
With rusted weathervane, a-twirl, a-swing,
My soul, better than in warm summer's bloom,
Will soar on raven's wing, vast, black of plume.

No pleasure like your shades to heart filled deep
With gloom, long blanketed with hoary rime,
O haggard seasons, queens of pallid clime,

—Unless it be to lull my pain to sleep,
On moonless nights, lying abreast, outspread
On some haphazard and precarious bed.

Le Crépuscule du matin

La diane chantait dans les cours des casernes,
Et le vent du matin soufflait sur les lanternes.

C'était l'heure où l'essaim des rêves malfaisants
Tord sur leurs oreillers les bruns adolescents;
Où, comme un œil sanglant qui palpite et qui bouge,
La lampe sur le jour fait une tache rouge;
Où l'âme, sous le poids du corps revêche et lourd,
Imite les combats de la lampe et du jour.
Comme un visage en pleurs que les brises essuient,
L'air est plein du frisson des choses qui s'enfuient,
Et l'homme est las d'écrire et la femme d'aimer.

Les maisons çà et là commençaient à fumer.
Les femmes de plaisir, la paupière livide,
Bouche ouverte, dormaient de leur sommeil stupide;
Les pauvresses, traînant leurs seins maigres et froids,
Soufflaient sur leurs tisons et soufflaient sur leurs doigts.
C'était l'heure où parmi le froid et la lésine
S'aggravent les douleurs des femmes en gésine;
Comme un sanglot coupé par un sang écumeux
Le chant du coq au loin déchirait l'air brumeux;
Une mer de brouillards baignait les édifices,
Et les agonisants dans le fond des hospices
Poussaient leur dernier râle en hoquets inégaux.
Les débauchés rentraient, brisés par leurs travaux.

L'aurore grelottante en robe rose et verte
S'avançait lentement sur la Seine déserte,
Et le sombre Paris, en se frottant les yeux,
Empoignait ses outils, vieillard laborieux.

Morning Twilight

The barracks echoed to the bugle's blare,
And lanterns flickered in the morning air.

It was the hour when nightmares swarm the heads
Of tawny youths, squirming about their beds;
When, like a darting, blinking, bloodshot eye,
The lamp burns red against the dawning sky;
And when, like vying sky and lamp, blithe soul
And surly body battle for control.
The air is full of myriad fleeting things
Taking their flight with fluttering of wings,
Like tear-strewn face, breeze-blown, wiped clean thereof.
Tired, poet quits his pen; woman, her love.

Here, there, the chimneys, one by one, began
To send their smoke aloft. The courtesan
And whore were lying, mouth agape, still deep
In their benighted, livid-lidded sleep.
Old crones, poor souls of frigid, sagging teat,
Puffed on their embers, blew the dying heat
Over their hands. It was the hour when those
In childbirth's pain know all too well the woes
Of chill distress. A distant chanticleer,
With blood-rent, sob-like crows, ripped through the blear
And mist-filled air: a sea of fog descending
Round and about; and those whose lives were ending,
Hospiced and bedded, gasped their agonies.
Rakes headed home, spent from their revelries.

Drear daybreak, quaking in her pink-green gown,
Inched up the barren Seine. Bleak Paris-town—
Sullen old workman—rubbed the sleep away,
Took up his tools, and faced another day.

Le Vin du solitaire

Le regard singulier d'une femme galante
Qui se glisse vers nous comme le rayon blanc
Que la lune onduleuse envoie au lac tremblant,
Quand elle y veut baigner sa beauté nonchalante;

Le dernier sac d'écus dans les doigts d'un joueur;
Un baiser libertin de la maigre Adeline;
Les sons d'une musique énervante et câline,
Semblable au cri lointain de l'humaine douleur,

Tout cela ne vaut pas, ô bouteille profonde,
Les baumes pénétrants que ta panse féconde
Garde au cœur altéré du poëte pieux;

Tu lui verses l'espoir, la jeunesse et la vie,
—Et l'orgueil, ce trésor de toute gueuserie,
Qui nous rend triomphants et semblables aux Dieux!

The Lone Man's Wine

The courtesan's especial glance—her air
That glides our way, as when the moon, a-shiver,
Sends down her beam over the lake, a-quiver,
To bathe therein her beauty devil-may-care;

A gambler's last few coins, clutched in his hand;
A kiss from Adeline, all skin and bones;
A wheedling tune, persistent, like the moans
And wails of human woes in distant land;

None of all that, O bottle deep, is worth
The pungent balms your belly's fertile girth
Holds for the pious poet's thirsting heart;

You pour out hope for us, and life, and youth,
—And pride, that boon that gilds the wretch uncouth
And sets us all, like conquering Gods, apart!

Le Vin des amants

Aujourd'hui l'espace est splendide!
Sans mors, sans éperons, sans bride,
Partons à cheval sur le vin
Pour un ciel féerique et divin!

Comme deux anges que torture
Une implacable calenture,
Dans le bleu cristal du matin
Suivons le mirage lointain!

Mollement balancés sur l'aile
Du tourbillon intelligent,
Dans un délire parallèle,

Ma sœur, côte à côte nageant,
Nous fuirons sans repos ni trêves
Vers le paradis de mes rêves!

Lovers' Wine

Splendid, today, the heaven above!
No bit, no spurs, no bridle... Love,
Let's gallop off, astride our wine,
To climes enchanted, realms divine!

Like angel pair, plagued, harried by
Heart's fevered madness, let us fly
Afar, through morning's crystal blue,
And follow our mirage! We two,

Floating abreast on the airy sea,
Lulled on the cunning whirlwind's wing,
Cradled in twofold ecstasy,

With neither rest nor respiting—
O soul mate, sister mine!—will flee
Off to my blissful fantasy.

La Destruction

Sans cesse à mes côtés s'agite le Démon;
Il nage autour de moi comme un air impalpable;
Je l'avale et le sens qui brûle mon poumon
Et l'emplit d'un désir éternel et coupable.

Parfois il prend, sachant mon grand amour de l'Art,
La forme de la plus séduisante des femmes,
Et, sous de spécieux prétextes de cafard,
Accoutume ma lèvre à des philtres infâmes.

Il me conduit ainsi, loin du regard de Dieu,
Haletant et brisé de fatigue, au milieu
Des plaines de l'Ennui, profondes et désertes,

Et jette dans mes yeux pleins de confusion
Des vêtements souillés, des blessures ouvertes,
Et l'appareil sanglant de la Destruction!

Destruction

Ever beside me, plying his vicious craft,
The Demon wafts about; discarnate gust
That I breathe in, suck down: foul devil-draught
That burns me, fills me with an endless lust.

Knowing my love of Art, at times he takes
A female form—alluring, splendorous—
And, with the false pretense of boredom, makes
My lips crave potions vile, iniquitous.

Far does he lead me from God's watchful eye,
Until, undone and breathless, here I lie
In this vast desert landscape of Ennui;

He flings before my muddled gaze, outspread,
Filthy old rags, wounds gaping raw and red,
And all Destruction's bloodied panoply!

La Débauche et la Mort sont deux aimables filles,

Prodigues de baisers

Les Deux Bonnes Sœurs

La Débauche et la Mort sont deux aimables filles,
Prodigues de baisers et riches de santé,
Dont le flanc toujours vierge et drapé de guenilles
Sous l'éternel labeur n'a jamais enfanté.

Au poëte sinistre, ennemi des familles,
Favori de l'enfer, courtisan mal renté,
Tombeaux et lupanars montrent sous leurs charmilles
Un lit que le remords n'a jamais fréquenté.

Et la bière et l'alcôve en blasphèmes fécondes
Nous offrent tour à tour, comme deux bonnes sœurs,
De terribles plaisirs et d'affreuses douceurs.

Quand veux-tu m'enterrer, Débauche aux bras immondes?
O Mort, quand viendras-tu, sa rivale en attraits,
Sur ses myrtes infects enter tes noirs cyprès?

The Two Good Sisters

Death and Debauch: good maids and hale; and oh,
So profligate of kiss! Tattered and worn
The rags that drape their virgin loins, which, though
They ever labor, yet have never borne.

Brothel and tomb, beneath their arbors, show
A couch impenitent, where naught but scorn
Moves the cursed poet: family's arch foe,
Hell's evil minion, sycophant forlorn.

Alcove and coffin, rich in blasphemy,
Offer us, each, as these good sisters do,
Fell pleasures, foul delights. Ah, when will you,

O fetid-armed Debauch, come bury me?
And, rival Death, when will you graft unto
Her odious myrtle your black cypress tree?

La Fontaine de sang

Il me semble parfois que mon sang coule à flots,
Ainsi qu'une fontaine aux rythmiques sanglots.
Je l'entends bien qui coule avec un long murmure,
Mais je me tâte en vain pour trouver la blessure.

A travers la cité, comme dans un champ clos,
Il s'en va, transformant les pavés en îlots,
Désaltérant la soif de chaque créature,
Et partout colorant en rouge la nature.

J'ai demandé souvent à des vins capiteux
D'endormir pour un jour la terreur qui me mine;
Le vin rend l'œil plus clair et l'oreille plus fine!

J'ai cherché dans l'amour un sommeil oublieux;
Mais l'amour n'est pour moi qu'un matelas d'aiguilles
Fait pour donner à boire à ces cruelles filles!

The Fountain of Blood

At times I seem to hear a throbbing flood,
A sobbing fountain, gushing with my blood.
I hear it rushing with a long, low sigh,
But never find the wound, hard though I try.

About the city, like a duelling-ground,
It turns the streets to islands, and spreads round,
Through nature's realm, its hue incarnadine,
Slaking the thirst of beasts that dwell therein.

I've often begged strong wines to lull my fear,
For but one day: my terrors, my travails.
For naught! Wine makes more keen my eye, my ear!

I've sought forgetful sleep in loving; but
For me, love is a pain-wrought bed of nails,
Whereon I let my whoring wenches glut!

Je vis en plein midi descendre sur ma tête

Un nuage funèbre et gros d'une tempête

La Béatrice

Dans des terrains cendreux, calcinés, sans verdure,
Comme je me plaignais un jour à la nature,
Et que de ma pensée, en vaguant au hasard,
J'aiguisais lentement sur mon cœur le poignard,
Je vis en plein midi descendre sur ma tête
Un nuage funèbre et gros d'une tempête,
Qui portait un troupeau de démons vicieux,
Semblables à des nains cruels et curieux.
A me considérer froidement ils se mirent,
Et, comme des passants sur un fou qu'ils admirent,
Je les entendis rire et chuchoter entre eux,
En échangeant maint signe et maint clignement d'yeux:

—"Contemplons à loisir cette caricature
Et cette ombre d'Hamlet imitant sa posture,
Le regard indécis et les cheveux au vent.
N'est-ce pas grand'pitié de voir ce bon vivant,
Ce gueux, cet histrion en vacances, ce drôle,
Parce qu'il sait jouer artistement son rôle,
Vouloir intéresser au chant de ses douleurs
Les aigles, les grillons, les ruisseaux et les fleurs,
Et même à nous, auteurs de ces vieilles rubriques,
Réciter en hurlant ses tirades publiques?"

J'aurais pu (mon orgueil aussi haut que les monts
Domine la nuée et le cri des démons)
Détourner simplement ma tête souveraine,
Si je n'eusse pas vu parmi leur troupe obscène,
Crime qui n'a pas fait chanceler le soleil!
La reine de mon cœur au regard nonpareil,
Qui riait avec eux de ma sombre détresse
Et leur versait parfois quelque sale caresse.

Beatrice Mine

One day, in ash-strewn, brown-burnt wastes, as I
Stood hurling my lament against the sky
And honing on my heart, deliberately,
My thought's sharp blade, in aimless vagary,
I saw above my head a deathly cloud,
Thick with storm's gloom, and teeming with a crowd
Of dwarfish demon creatures, cruel and vicious,
Glaring at me with that cold and malicious
Glower of passerby whose eye is caught
By some poor madman, lunatic distraught.
I heard them whisper, each to each, and saw
Them wink and nod, with many a wry guffaw:

—"Let's take our leisure," leered the evil chorus,
"And contemplate this parody before us:
Vision of Hamlet, with his tousled hair
Blown in the wind; his vacant, vapid stare!
Quaint wastrel, thespian at liberty!
Pitiful *bon vivant,* who arrantly
Presumes that, since he mouths so well his role,
All Nature yearns to see him bare his soul:
Eagles and crickets, streams and flowers; who seems
To feel that even we, who sired these schemes
Of his, desire to hear his hue and cry!"

My pride, however, rising mountain-high
Above that cloud (the clamoring demon horde),
I could have turned my haughty head, ignored
Their vulgar troupe, had I, alas, not seen,
There in their midst, my heart's delight; my queen,
She of the peerless glance—O crime that might
Have stayed the sun and turned my day to night!—
With vile caress hugging them chin to chin,
And laughing with them at my dark chagrin.

Abel et Caïn

Race d'Abel, dors, bois et mange;
Dieu te sourit complaisamment.

Race de Caïn, dans la fange
Rampe et meurs misérablement.

Race d'Abel, ton sacrifice
Flatte le nez du Séraphin!

Race de Caïn, ton supplice
Aura-t-il jamais une fin?

Race d'Abel, vois tes semailles
Et ton bétail venir à bien;

Race de Caïn, tes entrailles
Hurlent la faim comme un vieux chien.

Race d'Abel, chauffe ton ventre
A ton foyer patriarcal;

Race de Caïn, dans ton antre
Tremble de froid, pauvre chacal!

Race d'Abel, aime et pullule!
Ton or fait aussi des petits.

Race de Caïn, cœur qui brûle,
Prends garde à ces grands appétits.

Race d'Abel, tu croîs et broutes
Comme les punaises des bois!

Abel and Cain

Race of Abel, eat, drink, sleep;
God looks on with smiling eye.

Race of Cain, go forth, a-creep;
Slither through the muck, and die.

Race of Abel, Seraph's senses
Relish your self-sacrifice!

Race of Cain, must your offenses
Evermore exact their price?

Race of Abel, your flocks grow,
And your plantings' fruits abound.

Race of Cain, your belly's woe
Wails like starving, scurvy hound.

Race of Abel, bask and revel
In your hearth ancestral's heat;

Race of Cain, poor homeless devil,
Tremble in your chill retreat!

Race of Abel, procreate!
See your gold spawn young no less.

Race of Cain, avoid that great,
Greedy, burning lustfulness.

Race of Abel, how you spread,
As the fattening stinkbugs do!

Race de Caïn, sur les routes
Traîne ta famille aux abois.

II

Ah! race d'Abel, ta charogne
Engraissera le sol fumant!

Race de Caïn, ta besogne
N'est pas faite suffisamment;

Race d'Abel, voici ta honte:
Le fer est vaincu par l'épieu!

Race de Caïn, au ciel monte
Et sur la terre jette Dieu!

Race of Cain, you drag, half-dead,
Your sad brood along with you.

II

Ah! Your carrion, Abel's race,
Will enrich the steaming soil!

Race of Cain, still must you face
And complete your final toil;

Race of Abel, to your shame,
Plough has not the game-pike's worth!

Race of Cain, your place reclaim:
Rise to heaven, cast God to earth!

Mon esprit, comme mes vertèbres,

Invoque ardemment le repos

La Fin de la journée

Sous une lumière blafarde
Court, danse et se tord sans raison
La Vie, impudente et criarde.
Aussi, sitôt qu'à l'horizon

La nuit voluptueuse monte,
Apaisant tout, même la faim,
Effaçant tout, même la honte,
Le Poëte se dit: "Enfin!

Mon esprit, comme mes vertèbres,
Invoque ardemment le repos;
Le cœur plein de songes funèbres,

Je vais me coucher sur le dos
Et me rouler dans vos rideaux,
O rafraîchissantes ténèbres!"

The End of the Day

In all its raucous impudence
Life writhes, cavorts in pallid light,
With little cause or consequence;
And when, with darkling skies, the night

Casts over all its sensuous balm,
Quells hunger's pangs and, in like wise,
Quells shame beneath its pall of calm,
"Aha, at last!" the Poet sighs.

"My mind, my bones, yearn, clamoring
For sweet repose unburdening.
Heart full of dire, funereal thought,

I will lie out; your folds will cling
About me: veils of shadow wrought,
O darkness, cool and comforting!"

NOTES

TO THE READER (page 5)

line 10: Baudelaire is here ascribing to Satan the many talents—mystical, astrological, and especially alchemical—of the Egyptian god Thoth, known to Neoplatonists, among others, as Hermes Trismegistos, and generally equated in various respects with the Greek god Hermes.

THE SICK MUSE (page 15)

line 8: The reference is to the small town of Minturnae, in Latium, in whose swamps the popular Roman general Gaius Marius, conqueror of Jugurtha and the Teutons, eventually took refuge from his aristocratic rival Sulla.

line 13: My use of the word "rhyme" here is metaphorical, since, as the reader appreciates, the Ancients didn't use it in their poetry, one of the several realms of the god Phoebus (Apollo).

THE JINX (page 21)

line 14: Baudelaire's concluding tercets are an obvious recollection of lines in Thomas Gray's celebrated "Elegy Written in a Country Church-Yard," of a century before: "Full many a gem of purest ray serene, / The dark unfathom'd caves of ocean bear: / Full many a flower is born to blush unseen, / And waste its sweetness on the desert air."

DON JUAN IN HELL (page 29)

Title: The reader will appreciate that Baudelaire's allusion to elements of the Don Juan story bears heavily on Molière's five-act seriocomic treatment of the subject.

lines 2–4: In Greek mythology Charon was the oarsman who transported dead souls across the River Styx, whereas the flesh-and-blood philosopher Antisthenes, known for his renunciation of the pleasures of society and the flesh, and for his excessive attachment to a life of poverty, was a follower of Socrates and founder of the Cynics.

THE IDEAL (page 39)

line 5: Sulpice-Guillaume Chevalier, known as Gavarni, was a popular artist of the period, whose witty and socially satiric cartoons, not unlike those of Daumier in spirit and intent, often appeared in the review *Le Charivari*.

line 14: Baudelaire appears, by this suckling reference, to be under the impression that mythological Night was the mother of the Titans. Although a variety of traditional Greek mythologies all name Earth (Gaia) as their mother and Heaven (Ouranos) as their father, Antoine Adam, in his edition of *Les Fleurs du mal* (Paris: Garnier, 1959, p. 298), not only attributes the assumption to Baudelaire but also, curiously, asserts its accuracy: "Baudelaire connaît par des lithographies *La Nuit* de Michel-Ange, dans la chapelle des Médicis à Florence. Et il sait que, dans la mythologie grecque, la Nuit était mère des Titans." ("Through lithographs, Baudelaire knows Michelangelo's *Night*, in the Medici chapel in Florence. And he knows that, in Greek mythology, Night was the mother of the Titans.") As sister of Gaia—both were daughters of Chaos—Night (Nyx) would, one assumes, have been only the Titans' aunt.

"Tu mettrais l'univers... " (page 56)

Title: Many scholars assume that this poem was inspired by Baudelaire's first mistress, Sarah "la Louchette" (see p. 197).

Sed non satiata (page 59)

Title: Baudelaire's Latin title ("but she, not satisfied") approximates a phrase of Juvenal's, *necdum satiata* ("she, not yet satisfied"), in his description of the lascivious Messalina, wife of the Roman emperor Claudius (*Satires*, VI, 130). The "heroine" of this sonnet, in which some find lesbian connotations, is generally assumed to have been Jeanne Duval, though a case has also been made for Sarah "la Louchette" (see p. 197).

line 3: The allusion to a Faust figure—albiet one in vaguely African witch-doctor *(obi)* trappings—may well have been suggested to Baudelaire by Gérard de Nerval's celebrated translation of part of Goethe's work, published in 1827.

line 5: In addition to opium, with which he was not unfamiliar, Baudelaire cites two wines here: the South African Constance, which had become rare even before his time, and the more familiar Nuits-Saint-Georges of Burgundy.

lines 12–14: Besides calling up the mythological belief that the Styx flowed in nine rings around Hades, Baudelaire's metaphor suggests his lack of a longed-for (if unrealistic) sexual prowess. Such interpretation is confirmed by the last-line reference to Persephone (Proserpina), wife of Pluto and goddess of the underworld—albeit against her will—and spirit of nature's renewal as well as ruler of the three Furies, one of whom was the disputatious Megaera.

De profundis clamavi (page 63)

Title: The well-known phrase ("From the depths I cried out... ") that serves as the title of this poem—originally to be entitled "Spleen," like several others—is taken from the Vulgate version of Psalm 130. It is especially appropriate in that it figures also in Catholic liturgy, in the Office of the Dead.

"Une nuit que j'étais..." (page 69)

lines 1–4: This sonnet was inspired by one "Sarah," with whom Baudelaire, in 1840, had his first liaison. Her nickname, "la Louchette," would suggest several unpleasant characteristics, physical and moral. The "beauty" referred to, apostrophized in the two tercets, is supposed to have been his later mistress, Jeanne Duval, already in his thoughts if not yet in his bed.

Reversibility (page 85)

lines 22–23: The reference is to the biblical story (I Kings 1:1–4) in which a young woman, Abishag the Shunammite, is brought to lie with King David and comfort him in his old age.

Evening Harmony (page 89)

Title: This is one of the more celebrated examples in French—or any western literature—of the *pantoum* (or *pantun*), a fixed form, borrowed, with significant variation, from the Malayan. In it, as here, the second and fourth lines of each quatrain become the first and third of the succeeding one.

line 16: The monstrance, also called ostensorium or ostensory, is the flat, usually sunburst-shaped receptacle in which the consecrated Host is displayed to the congregants at the Catholic mass for their adoration.

Heavens' Haze (page 93)

line 14: My translation of Baudelaire's *vos* by "their" is occasioned by the fact that the English "your" distinguishes neither between the singular and plural nor between the familiar and the formal, and would do more injustice to his intent than my minor liberty.

The Beautiful Ship (page 98)

lines 29–30: It is not impossible, depending on the meaning of the noun *volant*, that Baudelaire is envisioning here a totally different image: that of the two legs of a player running back and forth under the shuttlecocks ("sous les volants qu'elles chassent...") in a game of badminton. All things considered, the interpretation I have chosen is, I think, the less abstruse.

Chat (page 105)

Title: The apparently one-sided nature of this "chat" is only one of several ambiguities in this curious sonnet, all of which my translation attempts to render intact.

For a Creole Lady (page 107)

Title: Contrary to common belief, "creole" in this sense refers to an individual of European ancestry born in the colonies. The lady in question, Emmeline Carcerac, was the wife of Baudelaire's host, M. Autard de Bragard, during the refractory youth's enforced voyage to the island of Mauritius. A tempting hypothesis that his use of the verb *connaître* ("to know") was a twenty-year-old's fantasy on the biblical sense of the word is negated by the fact that he made quite certain his hostess and her husband would see the poem.

Mœsta et Errabunda (page 109)

Title: Being a feminine form, the Latin title, which can be translated as "sad wanderer," apparently applies to the apostrophized "Agathe," whose actual identity—if, indeed, she ever had one—has, to my knowledge, never been determined.

line 16: Because of Baudelaire's idiosyncratic punctuation, it is not clear whether all of the succeeding lines are part of "Agathe's" imagined quotation, or if they represent, once again, the poet's own speech. I opt for the latter interpretation.

198

Cats (page 119)

line 7: Baudelaire's "L'Erèbe," Erebos, the subterranean passage to Hades and the equivalent of "the valley of the shadow of death," was personified in Greek mythology as the son of Chaos, brother of Nyx (the Night), and father of the River Styx and the Fates.

The Pipe (page 125)

lines 1–8: Given the atypical, almost playful quality of this sonnet, my rhyme scheme in the two quatrains—one used only sparingly by Baudelaire in his sonnets—is not wholly unwarranted.

A Fantastic Engraving (page 133)

Title: This poem was apparently inspired by an engraving of the eighteenth-century English artist John Hamilton Mortimer, "Death on a Pale Horse," itself probably influenced by one or more works of Albrecht Dürer. (See *Œuvres complètes de Baudelaire* [Paris: Le Club du Meilleur Livre, 1955], I: 1229.)

Spleen ("Pluviôse, irrité, contre la ville entière... ," page 139)

line 1: Pluviôse was the fifth month in the Republican calendar, running from the last week in January to the last week in February.

HEAUTONTIMOROUMENOS (page 155)

Title: Baudelaire's Greek title, meaning "the self-tormentor," is borrowed from a comedy of Terence. The object of his dedication, "J. G. F.," is no doubt the same woman (one assumes) to whom he dedicated his *Paradis artificiels,* but whose precise identity has defied researchers.

line 28: Interestingly, this line was inspired by the last line of Edgar Allan Poe's poem "The Haunted Palace," found in "The Fall of the House of Usher," but I have avoided an exact reproduction of the original.

THE SWAN (pages 161, 163)

Dedication: Baudelaire's dedication of this poem in December of 1859 was not only a mark of admiration for Hugo—an admiration reciprocated—but also a logical extension of its subject, the elder poet being at the time in his self-imposed exile on the Channel Islands.

line 4: After the fall of Troy and the death of Hector at the hands of Achilles, Andromache (Hector's widow) became the captive of Pyrrhos, Achilles' son, who, before his own death, awarded her to his brother Helenos. The latter, to assuage his unwilling spouse's homesickness, created for her a makeshift rivulet intended, unsuccessfully, to resemble the Simois of her native Troy.

lines 4–8: Baudelaire's reference is to the substantial rebuilding of Paris by the urbanist Baron Haussmann during the Second Empire. The new Place du Carrousel, a parade ground surrounded on three sides by the much expanded Louvre, replaced the clutter referred to in the next stanza.

lines 24–28: Some scholars (and translators) assume this to be a reference to Daedalus. Others, myself among them, see it as an allusion to Ovid's description of primal Man in the *Metamorphoses* (I: 84, 85): "All other animals look downward; Man / Alone, erect, can raise his face toward Heaven" (trans. Rolfe Humphries [Bloomington: Indiana University Press, 1955], p. 5]).

lines 51–52: It must be more than coincidental that Baudelaire ends his poem with a seeming allusion to the subject of Victor Hugo's lyric "Oceano nox": the fate of sailors lost at sea, and their gradual disappearance even from the memories of those left behind. The echo of Hugo's line 25 is especially clear: "On demande: —Où sont-ils? sont-ils rois dans quelque île?" ["We ask: 'Where are they now? Kings of some isle?'"].

THE LONE MAN'S WINE (page 171)

line 6: "Adeline" appears to have been a name made up for the occasion (and the rhyme).

THE FOUNTAIN OF BLOOD (page 181)

line 9: An apparent misprint in the first edition of *Les Fleurs du mal* (1857) rendered *capiteux,* traditionally used to describe wine, as *captieux* ("fraudulent"), replacing the variant *généreux* ("generous") of the original manuscript. The misreading, long perpetuated through succeeding editions, was corrected in the one used here, though it prevails in many that have followed it.

line 14: It has been suggested that the enigmatic *cruelles filles* ("cruel girls") is a reference to Death and Debauch of the preceding sonnet. (See *Les Fleurs du mal*, ed. Antoine Adam [Paris: Garnier, 1959], p. 414.) But it is hard to reconcile that interpretation with the poet's characterization of them as *aimables* ("likable") in the first line of that poem. In my version I attempt to skirt the problem.

BEATRICE MINE (page 185)

Title: The obvious reference is to the object of Dante's hopeless (and long idealized) love, the Florentine Beatrice Portinari.

ABEL AND CAIN (pages 187, 189)

line 22: Baudelaire's scorn for the complacent, wealthy "Race of Abel" is aptly expressed by his comparison of it to this foul-smelling insect, a prolific and voracious member of the *Pentatomidae* family.

line 30: For lack of a better one, I adopt Antoine Adam's reading of this very enigmatic (and variously interpreted) line, according to which the *fer* ("iron") in question is a ploughshare, and the *épieu* ("pike"), a hunting weapon (see *Les Fleurs du mal* [Paris: Garnier, 1959], p. 422); although the same respected editor's assertion that Baudelaire reverses the original Cain and Abel story in Genesis IV, by transforming the former's progeny into hunters and the latter's into farmers, does not really accord with Old Testament text. What is incontrovertible, however, is that his Cain is clearly a social dissenter, not merely the metaphysical Romantic rebel of the final couplet, while his Abel represents the smug, well-fed bourgeois around the time of the 1848 revolution.

Illustrator's Notes

Portrait of Baudelaire (page ii)

Baudelaire was photographed in at least five different formal sittings by his lifelong friend, Félix Tournachon Nadar (1820–1910). In his book of 1911, *Baudelaire intime*, Nadar describes their first meeting in the Luxembourg Gardens: " . . . a young man of medium height with a good figure, all in black except for a russet scarf, his coat scrupulously cut, excessively flared with a roll collar from which his head emerged like a bouquet from its wrappings. . . . In his hand was a pale pink—I repeat pink— glove, he carried his hat, made unnecessary by the superabundance of very black hair which fell to his shoulders—a mane like a waterfall." It may have been a memory of this first sighting that caused Nadar to pose Baudelaire, at least twice, wearing a well-cut overcoat, sometimes with little evidence of clothing underneath.

Other printmakers have created intaglio portraits of Baudelaire's compelling presence: Felix Bracquemond for the Second Edition of *Les Fleurs du mal*, Felicien Rops for the frontispiece of *Les Épaves,* and no less than Édouard Manet.

Don Juan in Hell (page 27)

In conceiving an image to portray Doña Elvira's character, I kept rereading Baude-laire's poem, but always returned to *Don Giovanni*, hoping that including Lorenzo da Ponte's lyrics to her great fourth act aria "Mi tradi quell'alma ingrata" would recall Mozart's music and, together with my drawing, illustrate the hopeless love-sickness that Baudelaire captures in four lines.

The Ideal (page 37)

Michelangelo's sculpture *Night* is an image in this poem and is portrayed directly in the illustration. I go on to use references to this sculpture as a visual *leitmotif* in other illustrations. Between the flank and bent arm of the figure is a mask, which appears as the face of Satan in "To the Reader" (p. 5) and as the man in the moon in both "The Vampire" (p. 67) and "The Incubus" (p. 113). The leg of *Night* and the owl under the crook of the knee in the sculpture return, appropriately, in "The Owls" (p. 123).

The Giantess (page 41)

While the landscape in this print is that of the mountains of North Carolina, where it was made, both the technique—subsequent open biting in successive baths after the line has itself been etched in successive baths—and the composition, particularly the whorls of hair, remember and pay homage to the prints of Max Klinger (1857– 1920).

ALL OF HER (page 77)

Whether this poem was in the mind of Jean-Luc Godard when he created the scene in his film *Le Mépris* (Contempt), where the camera plays over the body of Brigitte Bardot while the voice of her husband, played by Michel Piccoli, discusses his affection for its various parts, the similarity is so strong that it helped me find an image, as well as a sense of light, for illustrating Baudelaire's poem.

THE INCUBUS (page 111)

In this illustration not only does the mask from Michelangelo's *Night* appear as the man in the moon, but also the lower figure is based on Michelangelo's *Dawn*, the opposing figure in the Medici Chapel.

A FANTASTIC ENGRAVING (page 131)

The illustration is based on one of Albrecht Dürer's most famous prints, "The Four Horsemen," one of fifteen large woodcuts from *The Apocalypse*, his first major work, published with German and Latin texts in 1498, when Dürer was twenty-seven. While Dürer's print is a woodcut, my rendition of it here as background is actually etched, while my own figure of the pale horse and its pale rider is, appropriately to the title of Baudelaire's poem, engraved with a burin.

SPLEEN (page 137)

The image of the hands in this engraving was inspired by Nadar's portrait of Marceline Desbordes-Valmore (1785–1859) taken in 1857. The white lace ruffled cuffs are exactly as they are in the photograph, but there the hands are covered by fingerless gloves of black lace, which were worn no doubt in the sitter's effort to cover exactly the crone-like qualities that Baudelaire's poem requires. I used the pattern of this lace, instead, for the table cover. Desbordes-Valmore is herself remembered for a poem ("Ma chambre") about the room of an old lady; but just as she wears lace gloves in her photograph, she covers the pain of old age in sentiment.

BEATRICE MINE (page 183)

The demons in the cloud bear a passing resemblance to Notre Dame's gargoyles or more directly to their vivid renditions in Charles Meryon's etchings.

THE END OF THE DAY (page 191)

This image is a sequel to the opening illustration, "To The Reader" (p. 3). Baudelaire's body as a marionette has been replaced by a skeleton, and the face of Satan by the face of Baudelaire, drawn after a photograph by Etienne Carjat (1828–1906).

ACKNOWLEDGMENTS

The following translations in this collection have previously been published and are reprinted here with permission: "The Albatross," "The Enemy," "Beauty," "I worship you," and "Sorrows of the Moon" in *Delos* (1998); "Correspondences" and "The Former Life" in *Source*, no. 25 (1997), published by the Literary Division of the American Translators Association; "Dressed in her opalescent . . .," "De profundis clamavi," and "Poison" in *The Texas Review* 18, nos. 1–2 (spring/summer 1997); "Burial" and "The Lone Man's Wine" in *Partisan Review* 65, no. 1 (1988); and "The Cracked Bell" in *The Formalist* 8, no. 2 (fall/winter 1997).

INDEX OF TITLES AND FIRST LINES

205

206

209